Integrated Lessons

Integrated Lessons

Pronunciation and Grammar

TEACHER'S MANUAL

Brenda Prouser Imber and
Maria Guttentag Parker

Ann Arbor

THE UNIVERSITY OF MICHIGAN PRESS

To Rod, Bailie, Jason, and Thunder

Preface

Integrated Lessons: Pronunciation and Grammar (ILPG) is designed for classroom use with intermediate and advanced students of English. It can be used as a primary, developmental text for intermediate students in

- Adult Basic Education (ABE) courses for nonnative speakers,
- General Equivalency Diploma (GED, i.e., high school equivalency) courses for nonnative speakers, or
- intensive English as a Second Language (ESL) courses.

It can also be used as a supplementary text in advanced ABE, GED, or ESL courses for remedial work in

- grammar,
- pronunciation, and
- speaking and listening.

ILPG is especially useful for teachers who need lessons that can be developmental for some students and remedial for others in the same class.

ILPG's step-by-step lesson plan is both clear and flexible, which makes it especially easy for beginning teachers to use. At the same time, it allows more experienced teachers considerable freedom to extend, improvise, and adapt, as well as to incorporate their own materials. Specifically, *ILPG* includes

1. instruction in grammar concepts chosen for their relevance to pronunciation;
2. pronunciation instruction that is quickly understood and easily carried out by both teacher and students;
3. exercises that develop students' ability to integrate the practice of grammar and pronunciation into the context of their daily activities;

4. a teacher-student tutorial process that is simple, efficient, and effective; and

5. a feedback process that turns ESL students into knowledgeable peer tutors.

Acknowledgments

Many colleagues and students have contributed to this text. Specifically, we would like to thank Joan Morley for her expertise, support, and encouragement and especially for her vowel sound number system, which is central to this text; John Swales, Director of the English Language Institute (University of Michigan), for institutional support; Leslie Olsen, whose concern for her engineering students led to the original field-testing of the ideas in this text; Barry Chen, who combed the manuscript and made many constructive suggestions; and our many students who provided valuable feedback and helped field-test the lessons.

Contents

Symbols

Although you might want to create your own set of symbols for marking stress, linking, intonation, deletions, and phrasing, we have used the following:

Stress	—	(underlined syllable/word)
Linking	U	(between words)
Intonation	↗	(rising)
Deletion	\	(through letters)
Phrasing	//	(between word groups)
Becomes or changes to	➡	

For transliterations we suggest using:

θ for voiceless /th/

Th for voiced /th/

Sh for ʃ

Ch for tʃ

j for ʤ

To avoid confusion between the number *1* and the letter *l,* we use the capital letter L in transliterations.

Charts and Forms

Introduction

Is it grammar or is it pronunciation that makes a nonnative speaker hard to understand? To answer this question, consider this situation:

- Student A's pronunciation improves after instruction, but because of her many grammar errors she is still incomprehensible.
- Student B, on the other hand, has improved his grammatical accuracy, but remains unintelligible because of his pronunciation errors.

In these all too common cases, neither grammar nor pronunciation instruction alone has led to improved comprehensibility. This leads to the answer that it is not *either* grammar *or* pronunciation that weakens intelligibility, but both. The two components are integrated; they interact with and influence each other. So why teach them sequentially when integrating the two could bring more comprehensive improvement?

As ESL teachers look for ways to teach pronunciation as an integral part of oral communication courses, rather than as a separate component, a number of challenges emerge.

The first is the challenge of creating an ESL pronunciation syllabus that can be integrated into oral communication courses. *ILPG* responds to this challenge by providing a text that combines the teaching of pronunciation with the teaching of grammar within lessons that are relevant and specific to students' individual needs.

A second challenge is to provide materials and activities that are varied enough to address each learner's specific speech needs, which can be quite diverse within a single class. *ILPG*'s activities meet this challenge by providing exercises that are tightly structured yet require students to generate their own subject matter. Thus, while the focus is on individual grammar and pronunciation needs, the students can continue to work and practice as a class. Furthermore, the activities can be repeated without being boring. Since the students make up the content themselves (personal narratives, dialogues, anecdotes, etc.), each time an exercise is done, the content is different. However, the grammar and pronunciation points in question remain the same, thereby providing reinforcement and review.

A third challenge arises from the need to set specific goals for student achievement and to measure student progress. Teachers usually measure progress by checking that exercises have been completed and by discrete-point testing. However, this process does not always tell us how well students apply information outside the classroom. *ILPG* encourages students to draw on a variety of sources outside the text and the classroom, creating a format for practice through application in their own environments. This continual real-life application thus becomes the test of student progress.

In integrating pronunciation and grammar instruction, *ILPG* offers original and interesting ways to meet these challenges. Through a series of step-by-step lesson plans, the text and accompanying Student Workbook have been specifically created to address grammar areas that we have found to be frequently linked with pronunciation problems. Easy-to-follow grammar and pronunciation charts and activity sheets keep the focus on *how* to say *what* correctly. Teachers and students are provided with a unique opportunity to balance two vital areas of ESL instruction.

Suggested Readings

The following is a brief list of resources we have found particularly useful.

Collins Cobuild English Language Dictionary. London: Collins, 1987.

Gilbert, Judy B. *Clear Speech: Pronunciation and Comprehension in American English.* Cambridge: Cambridge University Press, 1984.

Kenyon, John S., and Thomas A. Knott. *A Pronouncing Dictionary of American English.* Springfield, MA: G. & C. Merriam Co., 1944.

Longman Dictionary of American English. New York: Longman, 1983.

Morley, Joan. *Improving Spoken English.* Ann Arbor: University of Michigan Press, 1979.

————. *Intensive Consonant Pronunciation Practice.* Ann Arbor: University of Michigan Press, 1992.

————. *Rapid Review of Vowel and Prosodic Contexts.* Ann Arbor: University of Michigan Press, 1992.

Morley, Joan, ed. *Current Perspectives on Pronunciation.* Washington, D.C.: TESOL, 1987. Several articles in this volume are especially recommended, namely: Marianne Celce-Murcia, "Teaching Pronunciation as Communication," 3–12; Rita Wong, "Learner Variables and Prepronunciation Considerations in Teaching Pronunciation," 15–28; Mary S. Temperley, "Linking and Deletion in Final Consonant Clusters," 59–82; J. C. Catford, "Phonetics and the Teaching of Pronunciation: A Systemic Description of English Phonology," 83–100.

Nilsen, Don, and Aileen Nilsen. *Pronunciation Contrasts in English.* New York: Regents Publishing Co., 1971.

Prator, Clifford H., and Betty W. Robinett. *Manual of American English Pronunciation.* 3d ed. New York: Holt, Rinehart and Winston, 1972.

Raimes, Ann. *How English Works: A Grammar Handbook with Readings.* New York: St. Martin's Press, 1990.

Steer, Jocelyn M., and Karen A. Carlisi. *The Advanced Grammar Book.* New York: Newbury House, 1991.

Guidelines

Many activities in *ILPG* are accompanied by specific charts, forms, or activity sheets. Instructions for their use are always included in the instructions for the activity, e.g., ''Turn to **#11 Modals.**'' Although activities marked [HMWK] are especially appropriate as homework assignments, they can also be done in class.

The active participation of imitating a model and actual production (rather than merely saying *yes* in passive acceptance) are essential to the development of both monitoring and self-monitoring skills. That is, when you correct errors, whether pronunciation or grammar, acknowledgment by the student is not sufficient. It is important to require students to *repeat* the word or phrase before continuing.

The activities in this book are based on the use of the Morley Vowel Sound Numbers system,* which is introduced in the first class. This system is easy to learn, easy to remember, and easy to use for both teacher and student. It quantifies vowel identification and practice and as such is invaluable in oral work. (A transition chart for students and teachers accustomed to using the IPA system is included with the Morley chart.)

Boxes labeled **FYI** provide additional information and suggestions. They do not appear in the *Student Workbook.*

---

* Found in Joan Morley, *Improving Spoken English* (Ann Arbor: University of Michigan Press, 1979).

Procedures

Two procedures are central to *ILPG*'s integration of pronunciation and grammar: the *tape-script exchange* and the *self/peer feedback* process.

Tape-Script Exchange

Establishing regular tutorial opportunities between student and teacher is one of the main focuses of *ILPG*. This interaction is accomplished through the exchange of tape recordings. Those exercises that lend themselves especially well to this procedure are marked as such.

Each student must have two audio tapes. (More than two becomes unwieldy and confusing.) This way it is possible to collect one assignment and return another on the same day. Use short tapes (fifteen to thirty minutes per side), since longer ones break too easily and require too much rewinding and searching.

A recording assignment consists of the student's tape plus a script, which is the student's written version of what he or she said.

The tape-script exchange consists of these steps:

- Assign an activity that requires a recording and a script.
- Collect tapes and scripts.
- When listening to a tape, follow along on the student's script. Do not try to mark all mispronunciations; concentrate on one or two vowel or consonant sounds per assignment.
- Use the script to re-record the text, leaving pauses for practice. Your corrections provide a model for pronunciation work.
- Mark grammatical corrections on the script. Limit them to the focus area of the activity (e.g., wrong use of *should* in a dialogue practicing modals).

- You might also want to record a few general remarks about pronunciation, grammar, speed or volume of speech, etc.
  Your recording thus individualizes corrections and serves as a guide for practice for each student.
- Provide listening practice, if desired, by *not* writing any of the corrections you make. Students can then be required to transcribe your corrected recording.
- Return tapes and scripts. Explain guided practice: that you have re-recorded the scripts, with pauses so the student can practice. Also explain that you have made some corrections and comments on the tape, the script, or both. The student uses your re-recording, corrections, and comments to get feedback.

Your entire time with one tape should be no more than five to ten minutes: one to two minutes listening to the original recording, marking the script as you listen; two to four minutes re-recording with pauses; two to three minutes making other comments. Short (under one minute) student recordings contain sufficient evidence of weaknesses and provide manageable practice segments.

Self/Peer Feedback

One major reason that corrections are not retained beyond the classroom is that students are unable to correct their errors until they can *hear* them, in their own speech as well as in that of others. Learning to listen in order to self-correct and to give peer feedback is the second major focus of *ILPG.* Each oral activity provides the opportunity for students to actively self-monitor and peer monitor the grammar and pronunciation points of the lesson. This monitoring means that during or after an activity, students discuss both their own and their peers' performance. The activity sheets in each lesson are structured to keep the focus narrow. This not only promotes monitoring but minimizes vague comments (such as "I thought it was very good"), which are flattering but not much help.

For any activity, you might proceed as follows:

- One student speaks. The others and the teacher make notes on the points in question.
- The speaker comments first on any problems she or he noticed, e.g., "I'm still having problems with *Th-,* like in 'brother'"; "I spoke too quickly"; "I said 'I bought computer' instead of 'I bought *a* computer.'"
  Then the other students comment, using the notes they have made.

- The teacher comments last, although he or she might wish to briefly reinforce or correct other comments as they occur. This order encourages both active student monitoring and effective peer feedback. It has the additional benefit of increasing students' credibility with each other as valid critics, particularly when the teacher reinforces their comments.

- All activities can include work on individual vowel and consonant problem sounds. Each student can choose one or two sounds to work on in addition to the specific focus areas of the activity. This enables students to tell their peers and the teacher which sounds to listen for.

To the Student

The activities in this workbook combine pronunciation and grammar. This combination will give you the opportunity to practice and improve both concurrently.

You will learn two procedures that are central to this integration of pronunciation and grammar: the *tape-script exchange* and *self/peer feedback.* Your teacher will explain the steps to you in detail.

Here are some guidelines for when you hand in a tape and a script:

1. On both the tape and the script, mark whether the recording is on side A or B. Before you hand in the tape, cue it to the point where the teacher is to begin listening. Do not rely on counter numbers.
2. When you hand in a dialogue script, put your name first, then your partner's name, at the top of the page. Always hand in your tape and script together with your partner's.
3. Do not tape over previous recordings.
4. Use only tapes that are thirty minutes or less per side. Longer ones are thinner and break more easily.

Lesson One

Pronunciation: Learning the Basics

Here is a step-by-step format for beginning instruction.

1. If you are using this book as a core text, on the first day of class, begin with a general introduction that includes information on the purpose of the class, organization, procedures, activities, and materials. Remind students that they will need tape recorders that can record as well as play.

2. Next, turn to **#1 Comprehensibility Quotient.** Ask students to read the descriptions (or explain them to the class yourself) and then mark where they think they fit on the chart. They may use nonwhole numbers, e.g., 2.75. Ask them to date the form and turn it in to you. Keep it until the end of the course, when the students will rate themselves again for a before-and-after comparison.

3. Turn to **#2 Consonant Sound Categories** and **#3 Consonants That Might Cause Problems.**

   - First, present a quick overview of all the sounds. Model each one by giving an example of a word in which it is used (e.g., **r**at, **f**ine, **th**ink).
   - Next, ask students to identify the sounds that are difficult for them (personal problem sounds) by circling them on the chart. This serves two purposes: it introduces the concept of self-monitoring and it individualizes instruction from the beginning.
   - Tell the class that each student will choose one or two identified problem sounds to work on within each activity. This makes students responsible for requesting feedback and modification on the sounds they are practicing. When you and the student agree that he or she can self-correct a given sound, the student can move on to other problem sounds in subsequent class activities.

FYI*

Students often know some of the things that are problematic for them, but they might not be used to an approach that asks them to do this kind of self-analysis. They might tell you that they are not sure what their problems are. In their view, as the teacher, *you're* supposed to tell *them*. However, learning to self-monitor is central to lasting improvement. For this reason, it is important to press students to identify at least one difficult consonant (and later, vowel) sound. You will, of course, suggest additional sounds as instruction proceeds. As students get used to giving and getting feedback, they will often modify their lists themselves. Furthermore, motivation is increased because students have a key role in identifying what they will study.

FYI = for your information

---

4. Turn to **#4 Morley American English Vowel Sounds plus International Phonetic Alphabet Symbols.**

   • Review the sixteen sounds.
   • Model each cue word individually and ask students to repeat it.
   • Then, as a class, begin to memorize the sounds, using the cue words as mnemonic aids:
      See it?
      1   2
      Say yes.
      3   4
      fat bird
      5   12
      bus stop   a fat bird at the bus stop
      6   7   16 5   12 5 16 6   7
      two books
      8   9
      no law
      10   11
      my cowboy
      13   14 15

When students have memorized the cue words in the order above, lead the class in repeating them, along with their corresponding numbers, e.g.,

"1–2, *see it;* 3–4, *say yes . . . ,*" or "*See it,* 1–2; *say yes,* 3–4 . . . ." To get students used to the correspondence between sound and number, ask them to generate several more cue-words for each vowel sound (VS). For instance, for VS #1, they might list *peace, piece,* and *seize;* for VS #12 they might list *were, fur, her,* and *heard;* for VS #8 they might list *food, threw, through, blue;* for VS #9 they might list *would, wood, push;* and so on.

As noted in the Guidelines, this system of vowel identification has several advantages:

- It takes only a few minutes to learn.
- It gives everyone a common system and eliminates the problem of different sets of phonetic symbols.
- It enables you to explain or modify pronunciation by comparing numbers, rather than having to write symbols on the board.
- It allows you to correct and adjust sounds by degrees. For instance, you can tell a student who is pronouncing *says* as *saze* (S3Z), "*Say* has VS #3, but *says* has VS #4." If that student then has difficulty with VS #4 itself, you can describe gradations of improvement quantitatively, e.g., "That's getting better; now it's about 3.5. Reach down a little more for 4." You could also make use of other relevant student knowledge, such as sharps and flats as in music.

Since corrections and comments use this vowel-sound number system, it is important that the students memorize the chart. As a study activity, have them pair off and quiz each other, e.g., "What's the word for vowel sound 5?" "fat"; "What vowel sound number is the word *bus*?" "6"; and so on.

5. Next, explain the transliteration system to be used. Briefly, in transliterating words, we

- write the appropriate vowel numbers for the vowel sounds, instead of the letters (for example, the word *bed* is written B4D and *bead* is written B1D);
- write the consonants as they sound, which is not always as they are spelled (for instance, *cat* is written as K5T, *nation* is written N3Sh16N); and
- do not write silent letters, whether vowels or consonants (thus, *write* is written R13T, *bright* is written BR13T, and *comb* is written K10M).

6. Turn to **#5 Spoken American English Vowel Sounds** for transliteration practice. You can make this a team competition or assign certain words to groups of students. After completing their transliterations, students read the words and phrases aloud. The dialogue below shows how you can correct pronunciation.

> Teacher: OK, the next one, 13 L2V H1R, what is it?
> Student: I leave here.
> Teacher: What's the second word, what vowel sound?
> Student: Sound #2, leave.
> Teacher: I'm hearing sound #1, leeeeeave; how should you say it with sound #2?
> Student: Oh . . . , leave . . . ok?
> Teacher: That's still too close to sound #1. Try reaching down toward #2. Or try leaving the vowel out; just say lv.
> Student: OK . . . live?
> Teacher: OK, that's closer.

As the course progresses, this kind of dialogue will occur between the students themselves. Those who feel ready to peer-monitor at this point should be encouraged to join the conversation.

As students themselves might notice, some words have more than one transliteration because of differences in individual pronunciation or in how a word is used. Some examples are

either	13Th12 or 1Th12
department	D2P7RTM16NT, D1P7RTM16NT, or D16P7RTM16NT
data	D3T16 or D5T16
envelope	4NV16L10P, 11NV16L10P, or 7NV16L10P
a	16 (as in a dog, a book, a car) or 3 (as in *a* dog, not several)

Students can collect other examples throughout the term.

7. For additional practice, continue wtih **#6 Spoken American English Vowel Sounds.** The activity can be continued by having groups think of expressions, transliterating them, and asking other groups to figure them out.

8. [HMWK]. Tell the students there will be a vowel-sound test at the beginning of the next class and that the only possible scores will be 100 percent or 0. Therefore, everyone should have the Morley Vowel Sound chart memorized by then.

9. [HMWK]. The following exercise introduces students to self-monitoring. They will write, transliterate, and audiotape themselves. These three modes of input help students visualize what they are saying or hearing, helping them learn to self-correct.

- Each student makes a list of five phrases that he or she uses frequently but finds difficult. These can be field-specific terms such as *mortgage adjustment* or personal information such as *I live at 892 Shipley Circle.*
- Next, the student asks a native speaker to model the phrases.
- Then the student writes the transliteration of the native speaker's pronunciation on **#7 Field-Specific Terminology.**
- The student now audiotapes each phrase, trying to imitate what he or she heard, using the transliteration as a guide.
- After taping, the student listens to his or her recording. Below the original (native speaker's) transliteration of each phrase, the student writes the transliteration of what he or she actually said.

This activity provides the students with a contrast for error analysis: while they might have transliterated the correct pronunciation, they might not have actually produced it. It also provides the teacher with information about what the student is able to hear. For instance, the entry might look like this:

Word or phrase	Vowel sound orthography
892 Shipley Circle	I heard
	3T N1**3**N T**8** Sh**2**PpL1 S1**2**K1**6**L
	I recorded
	5T N1**3** T**8** Sh**1**PpL1 S1**2**K1**6**L

Students will hand in both the tape and **#7** at the beginning of the next class. Do not expect students to be able to identify *all* their errors; the fact that they can find *any* shows them that self-monitoring is possible.

#1 Comprehensibility Quotient

Rating	Description	Impact on communication
1.0	Speech is reasonably intelligible, but pronunciation or grammatical errors distract listener; repetitions and verifications are frequently required.	Accent causes frequent interference with communication; significant listener effort required.
2.0	Speech is largely intelligible; pronunciation or grammar errors are obvious, but repetition and verification are less frequently required.	Accent causes interference primarily at the distraction level; listener's attention is often diverted from the content to focus instead on the novelty of the speech pattern.
3.0	Speech is fully intelligible; variances from native speaker norm are present, but repetition and verification are seldom required.	Accent causes little interference; speech is fully functional for effective communication; minimal listener effort required.
4.0	Speech is near native; only minor features of divergence from native speaker can be detected.	Accent causes no interference. Speech is fully comprehensible; no listener effort required.

Student's name _____

Native language _____

Self-rating _____   Date _____

Adapted from Joan Morley, *Intensive Consonant Pronunciation Practice* (Ann Arbor: University of Michigan Press, 1992).

1

#2 Consonant Sound Categories

Voiceless = without vocal cord vibration
Voiced = with vocal cord vibration

Stop sounds		Friction sounds		Stop + friction sounds	Nasal sounds	Glides
Voiceless	Voiced	Voiceless	Voiced	Voiced	Voiced	Voiced
p	b	f	v	tʃ (Ch) dʒ (J)	m	w
t	d	θ	Th		n	y
k	g	s	z		ŋ (ng)	l
		Sh	Zh			r
		h				

#3 Consonants That Might Cause Problems

Sounds	Hints
sh / tʃ / ts* ʃ + ʃ	try using a smile position
f / v	upper teeth touch lightly just inside the lower lip
p / b	close lips firmly over top and bottom teeth
l / n	middle of tongue is down for n
ŋ	front of the tongue is down; back of the tongue is up
s / z	upper and lower teeth are slightly separated and lips are spread add voicing to create z
r	raise the sides of the tongue for r

* Ts does not appear on #2 because it is not a single consonant, but a consonant combination.

#4 Morley American English Vowel Sounds
plus International Phonetic Alphabet Symbols

The following chart is adapted from Joan Morley's chart in *Improving Spoken English* (Ann Arbor: University of Michigan Press, 1979). It illustrates sixteen vowel sounds of American English via a number system that facilitates working with and writing the sounds of spoken English.

The International Phonetic Alphabet (IPA) symbols are included for those who prefer to use them as an aid in the transition from a known system to the new one.

The words serve as cues to aid in the memorization of the numbers.

The position of the numbers reflects the high-mid-low and front-central-back locations.

	Front		*Central*		*Back*	
High	1 see	i	12 bird	ɝ	8 two	u
	2 it	ɪ			9 books	ʊ
Mid	3 say	e	16 the	ə	10 no	o
	4 yes	ɛ	6 bus	ʌ		
Low	5 fat	æ	7 stop	ɑ	11 law	ɔ

Diphthongs

13 my	aɪ	14 cow	au	15 boy	ɔɪ

	Front	Central	Back
High	1 see	12 bird*	8 two
	2 it		9 books
Mid	3 say	16 the	10 no
	4 yes	6 bus	
Low	5 fat	7 stop	11 law

Diphthongs

13 my	14 cow	15 boy

---

* Vowels followed by the letter *r* are "colored" by the R sound. Throughout this text, we have transliterated all -R combinations with 12. However, the following can also be used:

-IR = 1R / 1-12 / 2-12	-ER = 3R / 3-12 / 4-12	-AR = 7R / 7-12	-ɔR = 11R / 11-12 / 10-12
ear, here, beer	air, wear, where	are, car, part	or, door, store

#5 Spoken American English Vowel Sounds
Listening and Pronunciation Practice

Use the chart on the left to help you pronounce the words in the first column. Then write them in the second column. Take turns pronouncing and listening. Use the last two blanks to make up your own; then test your partner.

American English Vowel Sounds

1 see	12 bird	8 two		
2 it		9 books		
3 say	16 the	10 no		
4 yes	6 bus			
5 fat	7 stop	11 law		

13 my	14 cow	15 boy

1. N3M   _____

2. Z2P K10D   _____

3. 16DR4S   _____

4. 2NSTR6KT12   _____

5. R4J16STR3Sh16N   _____

6. 13 L2V H1R   _____

7. 16N16Th12 W6N   _____

8. 5KS16D16NT   _____

9. Th1 16M12J2NS1 R8M   _____

10. Sh7P1Ng S4NT12   _____

11. _____   _____

12. _____   _____

#5a Spoken American English Vowel Sounds: Teacher's Answer Key
Listening and Pronunciation Practice

Use the chart on the left to help you pronounce the words in the first column. Then write them in the second column. Take turns pronouncing and listening. Use the last two blanks to make up your own; then test your partner.

American English Vowel Sounds

1 see	12 bird	8 two
2 it		9 books
3 say	16 the	10 no
4 yes	6 bus	
5 fat	7 stop	11 law

13 my	14 cow	15 boy

1. N3M — name

2. Z2P K10D — zip code

3. 16DR4S — address

4. 2NSTR6KT12 — instructor

5. R4J16STR3Sh16N — registration

6. 13 L2V H1R — I live here.

7. 16N16Th12 W6N — another one

8. 5KS16D16NT — accident

9. Th1 16M12J2NS1 R8M — the emergency room

10. Sh7P1Ng S4NT12 — shopping center

11. _____   _____

12. _____   _____

#6 Spoken American English Vowel Sounds
Listening and Pronunciation Practice

Use the chart on the left to help you pronounce the words in the first column. Then write them in the second column. Take turns pronouncing and listening. Use the last two blanks to make up your own; then test your partner.

American English Vowel Sounds

1	see	12	bird	8	two
2	it			9	books
3	say	16	the	10	no
4	yes	6	bus		
5	fat	7	stop	11	law

13	my	14	cow	15	boy

1. 1L4KTR10M5GN4D2K   _____

2. M5KR10-4K16N7M2K Th1-16R1   _____

3. PR10GR5M2Ng L5NgW16J   _____

4. N15Z P16L8Sh16N   _____

5. K4M16STR1 D16P7RTM16NT   _____

6. K16N13 H4LPY8   _____

7. L4TSG10 T16Th16M8V1Z   _____

8. W12K12Z K7MP16NS3Sh16N   _____

9. 13M S7R1 13M L3T   _____

10. 5T16B14D16L4V16N Th12D1   _____

11. _____   _____

12. _____   _____

#6a Spoken American English Vowel Sounds: Teacher's Answer Key
Listening and Pronunciation Practice

Use the chart on the left to help you pronounce the words in the first column. Then write them in the second column. Take turns pronouncing and listening. Use the last two blanks to make up your own; then test your partner.

American English Vowel Sounds

1 see	12 bird	8 two	
2 it		9 books	
3 say	16 the	10 no	
4 yes	6 bus		
5 fat	7 stop	11 law	

13 my	14 cow	15 boy

1. 1L4KTR10M5GN4D2K — electromagnetic

2. M5KR10-4K16N7M2K θ1-16R1 — macroeconomic theory

3. PR10GR5M2Ng L5NgW16J — programming language

4. N15Z P16L8Sh16N — noise pollution

5. K4M16STR1 D16P7RTM16NT — chemistry department

6. K16N13 H4LPY8 — Can I help you?

7. L4TSG10 T16Th16M80V1Z — Let's go to the movies.

8. W12K12Z K7MP16S3Sh16N — worker's compensation

9. 13M S7R1 13M L3T — I'm sorry I'm late.

10. 5T16B14D16L4V16N θ12D1 — at about eleven thirty

11. _____ _____

12. _____ _____

#7 Field-Specific Terminology

Name _____ Date _____

In column one, list five words or phrases that occur frequently in your
profession, occupation, or everyday life. Ask a variety of American
colleagues or friends to pronounce them. Then in column two, use the
vowel sound orthography to write a representation of what you heard.
Practice and then record the phrases.

Word or phrase   **Vowel sound orthography**

1.   I heard:

_____   I recorded: _____

2.   I heard:

_____   I recorded: _____

3.   I heard:

_____   I recorded: _____

4.   I heard:

_____   I recorded: _____

5.   I heard:

_____   I recorded: _____

Dialogue Practice

A: What's one of the terms from your field?

B: One of the terms from my field is _____.

A: Is that a hard one to say?

B: Yes, _____ is quite difficult. *or*

No, not really. _____ is pretty easy for me.

A: Let's hear it again.

B: OK. The term is _____ .

#8 American English Vowel Sounds Test

Name _____ Date _____ Score: 0/100%

Please diagram the Morley vowel sound number system. Be sure that:

- the numbers correspond to the correct cue word,
- your cue words are correctly spelled,
- all entries are in the correct boxes.

	Front	Central	Back
High			
Mid			
Low			

Diphthongs

Lesson Two

Prosodics: Stress, Rhythm, Intonation, Linking, Reduction, and Deletion

1. Collect **#7 Field-Specific Terminology** and tapes. Listen to each tape and read along on the student's activity sheet. Mark errors; then re-record the words and phrases, making changes and adding comments where appropriate. [Review Tape-Script Exchange, page 7, for a detailed description of this process.] You can also add general comments if you wish, such as, ''I notice that your vowel sounds #3 and #5 sound very similar. Try to make them more distinct; listen . . .'' [model the sounds and the words in which the student has used them].

2. **#8 American English Vowel Sounds Test.** Give students about five minutes to fill in the cue words and numbers. The only possible scores are 100 percent or 0. Tests can be handed in or used as a review exercise in class. In the latter case, students exchange papers. Those who think the test they have received is 100 percent correct can copy it onto the board. Any necessary corrections are made to the entries on the board; students then use these models to correct each other's tests.

3. Introduce stress, rhythm, intonation, linking, reduction, and deletion (which are often referred to as *prosodics* or *suprasegmentals*). Use **#9 Prosodics:** *How much wood would a woodchuck chuck if a woodchuck could chuck wood?*

   • Ask students to read the sentence to themselves and to enter numbers for all vowel sounds.
   • When all have finished, ask a few to read their versions to the class.
   • Next, model the prosodics yourself by reading the entire sentence aloud.*

---

*Native speakers commonly use the following stress pattern for this popular tongue twister:

How much **wood** would a woodchuck **chuck** if a **wood**chuck **could** chuck wood?

29

- Now model the sentence phrase by phrase and have the class repeat each phrase:

  How much wood   would a woodchuck chuck   if a
  woodchuck   could chuck   wood?
  Repeat several times.

- Model the entire sentence again and have students say it along with you, trying to achieve unison.
- After this practice, students should look back at the vowel sounds they have written and make any necessary changes. For instance, they frequently write 3 for the word *a,* which is actually reduced to 16 in this context because it is unstressed and linked to the preceding and following words.

4. Now discuss the concepts of stress, rhythm, intonation, linking, reduction, and deletion as described on **#9 Prosodics.**

5. Emphasize that these aspects of pronunciation, which form the melody of speech, are as important as the individual vowel and consonant sounds. Several examples can be used to illustrate the significance of melody and phrasing in speech comprehension:

   - Hum ''Happy Birthday'' and ask students if they heard the words in their minds as the melody was hummed. Hearing the melody evokes the words; if the melody were not recognizable, the words would not jump to our minds.
   - If you hear a television or radio turned down so low that you cannot understand the words, the prosodics allow you to recognize that English is being spoken.*
   - A sentence with incorrect intonation can cause more listener confusion than a misarticulated vowel or consonant. For example, the sentence *I don't have any idea,* spoken with stress placed on *have* and the first syllable of *idea* and a sentence-ending pause after *have* would look like this:

     I don't <u>have</u> [pause] any <u>idea</u>.

   By contrast, this same sentence with the correct intonation pattern but with vowel and consonant errors would look like this:

---

*This technique has also been suggested by others, e.g., Virginia French Allen and Judy Gilbert.

13 D8NT H7F 5N1 13D1-16.
(I doon't hoff any idea.)

Clearly, vowel and consonant errors do cause miscommunication. However, misplaced stress tends to interfere more with comprehensibility because the unfamiliar speech melody requires greater effort on the part of the listener.

6. Emphasize that approximating native speaker prosodics is a major factor in improving intelligibility, since we use these features to help understand a spoken message. For example, rising intonation at the end of the sentence *Are you busy?* tells us we are hearing a question.

Read the following sentence aloud. Direct the class to listen for the linking, reductions, and sentence stress.

> *Can I* smoke? is said KN13SM10K. Note the reduction of *can I* to KN13.

Next, read the response:

> ''You can, but I wish you wouldn't.

Discuss the absence of linking and reduction between *can* and *you* since *can* is stressed and separated from the preceding word.

Use the following sentences for discussion and practice.

- ''Can I help you?''
- ''I can't help you.''
- ''Could you help me?''
- ''Not now, but I can help you later.''
- ''I could go to the movies or to the beach.''
- ''I could go to the beach, but I'd rather not.''
- ''I don't have to read this book, but I might do it anyway.''
- ''I have to read this book fast because it's overdue.''

7. [HMWK] **#10 Prosodics Exercise.** Students mark some instances of stress, linking, reduction, and deletion in the passage. **#10a Prosodics Answer Sheet** shows one answer version; variations are possible. (Students should not try to mark *all* instances since it becomes overwhelming.)

#9 Prosodics

How much wood would a woodchuck chuck if a woodchuck could chuck wood?

Stress: The strength or energy with which a syllable in a word, or a word in a phrase, is pronounced relative to others. There are two kinds of stress, *syllable stress* and *word stress*.

Syllable stress: Generally, the syllable that is stressed in a word is fixed. For example, in the word *visited* the stress is always on the first syllable.*

Word stress: In contrast, word stress (also called *phrase* or *sentence stress*) is not fixed. It changes according to the intended meaning. In the sentence *I visited him* the stress can be on *I*, *visited*, or *him*, depending on what the speaker wants the sentence to mean.

Rhythm: The orderly alternation of stronger and weaker parts of sentences with a relatively regular recurrence of the strongest stresses in connected speech. English rhythm is stress-timed, which means that stress occurs at more or less regular intervals, with any number of syllables possible between the stresses. In the two sentences below, the intervals between the stressed words are essentially the same. Thus, in the second sentence the word groups between the stresses are reduced more (see **Reduction**, below):

> People like food.
> Many people that I know like to eat unusual food.

Intonation: The melody or tune of a language; a pattern of rising and falling pitch changes spreading across the length of a phrase group or sentence. For example, intonation is used to differentiate a question from a statement.

Linking: Connecting the end of one word and the beginning of the next. Words are not pronounced as separate units but linked in phrases with smooth connections and no pauses until the end of the phrase. For instance, the phrase *Is it right?* is said 2Z16T R13T?

Reduction: Weak pronunciation of unstressed parts of a word or phrase; sometimes drastically reduced to vowel sound #16 (schwa); as in W3T 16 M2N16T (wait a minute).

Deletion: Omission of a vowel after a stressed syllable. This omission occurs if a stressed syllable is followed by two unstressed syllables, especially when a vowel is followed by a single vocalic or nasal sound such as L, R, or N (vegetable, family, different, interesting, Wednesday).

---

* Words such as *produce* / *produce* or *content* / *content* have two stress patterns and thus seem to be exceptions. However, *produce* as a verb is always stressed on the second syllable and *produce* as a noun is always stressed on the first syllable. Thus, even in these seeming exceptions syllable stress is fixed. Lesson 10: Words with Stress Change includes words of this type.

#10 Prosodics Exercise

Name _____ Date _____

In the text below, mark instances of stress, linking, reduction, and deletion.
Use the following to indicate

stress	underline the stressed word
linking	show a connection
reduction	put a dot
deletion	cross out the vowel

I'm a part-time student. I do translating work at home to pay my tuition.
My apartment, where I work and study, is on the first floor. Until recently,
this was a very convenient situation. Over the past few weeks, however,
it had become inconvenient. There had been constant loud music coming
from the apartment above. Since I work during the day and study at
night, the noise was really a nuisance. So finally last evening, I decided
to go upstairs to 2-A and complain. The woman who answered the door
was friendly but confused. ''I don't know what you're talking about,''
she said. ''I just moved in and don't even have a radio yet. The only thing I
have that makes noise is my alarm clock.'' Now I was confused, because I
was sure I wasn't imagining it. Just then the door to 2-B opened and a man
stepped out carrying a cello. ''What seems to be the problem?'' he asked.
When I told him about the noise, he said, ''I'm the one you're looking
for. I've been practicing around the clock for an audition.'' ''Well, now that
the mystery is solved, let's see if we can solve the problem,'' I replied.
''I can understand that you need to practice, but could you limit your
practicing to a more reasonable schedule?'' ''How about if you give me
your class schedule, and I'll do my loudest practicing during those hours,''
he suggested. I agreed to give it a try, and today I worked and studied
to the soft sounds of a cello.

#10a Prosodics Exercise Answer Sheet

Here are some possible markings.

I'm a part-time student. I do *translating* work at *home* to pay my *tuition.*
My *apartment,* where I *work* and *study,* is on the *first floor.* Until *recently,*
this was a very convenient *situation.* Over the *past* few weeks, *however,*
it had become *inconvenient.* There had been *constant* loud *music coming*
from the apartment *above.* Since I *work* during the *day* and *study* at
night, the *noise* was really a *nuisance.* So *finally* last evening, I *decided*
to go upstairs to *2-A* and *complain.* The woman who answered the *door*
was *friendly* but *confused.* ''I don't know what you're *talking* about,''
she *said.* ''I just moved *in* and don't even have a *radio* yet. The *only* thing I
have that makes *noise* is my *alarm* clock.'' Now *I* was confused, because I
was *sure* I wasn't *imagining* it. Just *then* the door to *2-B* opened and a man
stepped *out* carrying a *cello.* ''What *seems* to be the *problem?*'' he *asked.*
When I *told* him about the *noise,* he *said,* ''I'm the one you're looking
for. I've been *practicing* around the *clock* for an *audition.*'' ''*Well,* now that
the *mystery* is solved, let's *see* if we can solve the *problem,*'' I *replied.*
''I can *understand* that you need to *practice,* but could you *limit* your
practicing to a more *reasonable schedule?*'' ''*How* about if you give me
your *class schedule,* and I'll do my *loudest* practicing during *those* hours,''
he *suggested.* I *agreed* to give it a *try,* and *today* I *worked* and *studied*
to the *soft* sounds of a *cello.*

Lesson Three

Modals

1. Divide the class into groups of three or four. Ask each group to choose one version of the passage done as homework (**#10 Prosodics Exercise**) and present it to the class, taking turns reading the sentences to show the markings they have agreed on. Discuss variations among the versions. Illustrate that some variations are acceptable according to intended meaning while others are not possible.

2. Go back to the sentences used in lesson 2:

   • <u>Can</u> I smoke? You <u>can</u>, but I wish you <u>wouldn't</u>.
   • <u>Can</u> I help you?
   • I <u>can't</u> help you.
   • <u>Could</u> you help me?
   • Not now, but I <u>can</u> help you later.
   • I <u>could</u> go to the movies, or the beach.
   • I <u>could</u> go to the beach, but I'd <u>better not</u>.
   • I don't <u>have to</u> read this book, but I <u>might</u> do it anyway.
   • I <u>have to</u> read this book fast because it's overdue.

   Add a few more:

   • I <u>might</u> go to the party tonight, but I really <u>should</u> study.
   • <u>Would</u> you ever go skydiving?

   This time discuss the modals and their meanings. Guide the students toward finding patterns of possibility, advisability, and other modal functions by asking questions such as "What's the difference between '**Can** I smoke?' and '**May** I smoke?' or between 'I **can't** help you' and 'I **can** help you'?" (You can also use "I **would** if I **could**, but I **can't** so I **won't**.") This activity can be extended by asking the students to contribute additional sentences.

35

3. Turn to **#11 Modals Chart.** Using the examples, discuss both meaning and pronunciation.

4. **#12 Modal Pronunciation Guide** is an opportunity for nonnative speakers to teach pronunciation. Students work in small groups; each group chooses several modals from the list. Using and adding to the hints, they practice the articulation of the words. *Have to* and *ought to* are done as examples. After groups have completed their preparation, each group teaches its list to the class.

5. [HMWK]. Ask students to use the modals on **#11 Modals** to make short sentences. For each sentence they should transliterate the phrase that contains the modal and mark phrase stress, reductions, and linking. If the class is large, specific modals can be assigned to individual students.

6. **FYI** is suggested for use as a quiz or test. It is not numbered since it is not included in the student workbook.

#11 Modals Chart

Verbs that are used to indicate advisability, capability, possibility, probability, expectation, prediction, or obligation; also to seek permission; to make requests and suggestions; or to express plans, etc.

Verb	Pronunciation	Explanation
can	K5N	Present ability or inability; used informally instead of *may;* can + not →K5NT.
could	K9D	Past tense of *can;* present or future permission; present possibility; also used in making requests; used with *if* to express the conditional; could + have →K9D16V; could + not →K9D16NT.
had better	H5D B4D12	Advice; suggestion; (pronoun) + had better →e.g., (Th3D) B4D12.
have to	H5FT16	Necessary; obligatory; same as *must;* colloquial got to →G7D16.
may	M3	Permission; allowed to; possibility; may + have →M3Y16V.
might	M13T	Possibility; *might + have* →M13T16V; might + not →M13TN11T (M13T16NT).
must	M6ST	Same as *have to; must + have* →M6ST6V; must + not →M6S16NT; must + not + have →M6S16NT16V.
ought to	11D16	A good idea, advising but not obligatory; probability; an expectation; same as *should.*
shall	SH5L	Extremely formal; infrequently used in spoken American English except in questions with the pronouns *I* and *we.*
should	SH9D	Same as *ought to;* probability; expectation; advice; should + have →SH9D16V; should + not →SH9D16NT; should + not + have →SH9D16NT16V.
will	W2L	Promising; requesting; *will + not* →W10NT.
would	W9D	Possibility; past tense of *will;* would + have →W9D16V; would + not →W9D16NT; would + not + have →W9D16NT16V.

#12 Modal Pronunciation Guide

Here are some notes that can help you pronounce the modals in context. You can also add some diagrams for those that continue to pose problems for you. Space is provided for you to add your own notes.

Modals	Hints
can	Use vowel sound #16 unless *can* is stressed.
could	*d* is voiced.
had better	H16DB4D12—*tt* pronounced as a *flapped d*.
have to	*v* sounds like *f*.
may	Stretch vowel sound #3.
might	Stretch vowel sound #13.
must	Remember to say both sounds *s* and *t* at the end. If followed by a word beginning with a vowel, *t* is usually a *flapped d*.
ought to	Can be either vowel sound #7 or #11. *t* is a *flapped d*.
should	Voiced at the end.
will	Make the *L* in the front of the mouth.
would	*d* is voiced.

What's Wrong?

Instructions: Correct the modal errors.

1. You're taking seven classes?

   I think you might be very smart!

2. When American students enter the university, they shouldn't have a major.

   Oh, but I thought that by the junior year they should have one.

3. Did you visit your parents this past weekend?

   No, I can't because I should study.

4. Are you going to the party?

   No, I must to study for an exam.

5. Where were you?

   The elevator was stuck and I should wait for an hour before I could get out.

Lesson Four

If + Would/Could

1. Have students put their sentences done as homework on the board and read them aloud. Discuss meanings and the use of stress, reduction, and linking.

2. Turn to **#13 *If + Would/Could* Conditional.** Explain the use of these modals:

   - past tense for hypothetical present (*If I knew . . .*)
   - past perfect for hypothetical past (*If I had known . . .*)

   As a class, practice the examples, marking vowel sound numbers, stress, linking, and reduction. Have students substitute new *if* clauses, e.g.,

   > I would buy that BMW
   >> if it were yellow.
   >> if it were for sale.
   >> if it weren't so rusty.

   Repeat this for the hypothetical past. Then have students pair up to make up some new sentences and present them to the class for critique.

3. Divide the class into small groups. (Refer to **FYI.**) Turn to **#14 Modals and Meaning.** Using the first sentence, instruct each group to

   - have one group member read the sentence aloud;
   - transliterate the sentence exactly as the speaker said it;
   - mark linking and underline the stressed words; and
   - paraphrase the sentence (tell what it means).

   Have each group report to the class; compare versions. Follow this with a discussion of how changes in stress create changes in meaning.

FYI

1. Before dividing into groups, work through the example at the top of the worksheet.

2. Then let the students do the first sentences as assigned.

   - Could you come at eleven?
     K6D J16 K6M 16D <u>16L4V16N</u>?
     (Is *this time* possible?)

   This reading of the sentence conveys the most general meaning; the idea of possibility is carried by the modal *could*. The stress is on *eleven* primarily because it follows the general intonation pattern of stress on the last content word in a sentence. (The stress on *eleven* would have to be even stronger if it were intended as a contrast to ten, nine, twelve, etc.)

   When the stress is shifted to a different word, the meaning also changes:

   - <u>Could</u> you come at eleven? (Is it <u>possible</u>?)
   - Could <u>you</u> come at eleven? (not someone else)
   - Could you come <u>at</u> eleven? (not before or after)

---

4. Continue in groups sentence by sentence, repeating the procedure: reading, transliterating, marking, paraphrasing, and reporting out. Then, as before, have the class discuss variations among the versions. The students then practice shifting the stress to other words to change the meaning of the sentence. They enter at least one variation for each sentence on **#14 Modals and Meaning**.

5. Each group then creates five to ten more sentences, including transliteration and intended meaning, writing them on **#15 Modals and Meaning Group Sentences**.

6. [HMWK]. Each student records five sentences from **#14 Modals and Meaning** and five from **#15 Modals and Meaning Group Sentences** and submits the recording with the worksheets. Students must indicate on the worksheets which sentences they have selected for recording.

Additional Activities

The following activities do not require worksheets.

1. Students can present original sentences to the class for discussion as follows:

Speaker:	''*I* can't help you.'' What is my intention?
Class member A:	You mean *you* can't help me. But maybe he can.
Speaker:	Anybody else?
Class member B:	I think you meant you can't help *me*. Maybe you can help *him*.
Teacher [to class]:	Who agrees with A? With B? Speaker, what was your intended meaning?
Speaker:	I personally can't help. Like A said.

If most of the class perceived the intended meaning correctly, solicit specifics on how this was done successfully (e.g., through emphasis on a particular word, apologetic look, strong voice, smile). If not, solicit suggestions about what the speaker could do to convey the intended message.

2. [HMWK]. Give students the following assignment to use for a tape-script exchange:

With a partner, choose one of the situations below and write a short dialogue (one or two minutes) using some of the modals we have studied. After you have created the dialogue, write it out (both partners should have a copy) and practice it. Then record your dialogue on each partner's tape. Hand it in next time, along with the written copy.

Situations:

1. You are talking with your friend at a party when you notice that a person you dislike has arrived.
2. You deposited a large amount of money in your account yesterday, but today the bank teller has just told you that your checking account is overdrawn.
3. Your car has just been serviced, and you are trying to find out from the mechanic how to figure out the bill.
4. You have finished taking your driving test, and you are asking the officer about your performance.

5. The landlord or apartment manager has finally returned your call about some problems you've been having.
6. Any situation from your own day-to-day life (a conversation at work, with your academic advisor, etc.).

You can also do this assignment alone, describing one of the above situations or a narrative responding to the following situation.

You were invited to dinner and brought flowers and a box of chocolates. Your hostess said, "Oh, you really shouldn't have." Describe what she meant and how you responded.

Again, write out your text, practice it, and then record it. Keep the narrative to a maximum of two minutes.

#13 Using *If + Could* or *Would* to Express the Conditional

If + Could / Would is used to talk about imagined or hypothetical situations.

Time	Main clause	*If* clause
Present	Structure: *could / would* + the regular form	Structure: past tense
	I would buy that BMW	if I had the money.
	I could find it	if I knew where it was.

Practice Clauses: Use vowel sound numbers and indicate linking.

1. _____

2. _____

3. _____

4. _____

5. (use negative)

Past	Structure: *could have / would have* + past participle	Structure: past perfect
	I could have passed the test	if I had studied harder.
	I would have won the money	if I had picked the right numbers.

Practice Clauses: Use vowel sound numbers and indicate linking.

1. _____

2. _____

3. _____

4. _____

5. (use negative)

#14 Modals and Meaning

Sentence	Transliteration	Meaning
Example: He shouldn't be doing that.	H1 Sh9D16NT B1 D8W1Ng Th5T Variations: **H1** Sh9D16NT B1 D8W1Ng Th5T H1 Sh9D16NT B1 **D8W1Ng** Th5T	Opinion statement: it is wrong / not good. He, as opposed to someone else Emphasis on stopping the action
1. Could you come at eleven?		
2. I have to be there by ten.		
3. I should be there by Monday.		
4. They must have known.		
5. I ought to be able to handle it.		
6. We'd better study for the test.		
7. She might be able to fix it.		
8. Who knows what he would have done.		

#15 Modals and Meaning Group Sentences

Sentence	Transliteration	Meaning

Lesson Five

Wish and *Hope*

1. Turn to **#16 What to Do with *Wish* and *Hope*.**

2. Discuss how and when to use *wish* and *hope.* Then ask students to provide additional examples for each category and enter them in the appropriate boxes.

3. Continue with **#17 *Wish* and *Hope* Notes and Practice.** First, using the transliterations, the class works together to develop pronunciation hints. One student might draw a diagram on the board of how to pronounce *wish* (a simple mouth diagram suffices). Other students can modify the drawing until all agree on it. Discuss the notes for *wish* and have students practice the sentences—marking linking, stress, and vowel sound numbers. Repeat this procedure for *hope.*

4. Divide the class into small groups. Each group now creates practice sentences for the tenses listed at the bottom of the page, marking linking and stress. Note that for the past progressive and past tenses there will be both a *wish* and a *hope* sentence. Each group presents its sentences for these two tenses to the class for critique.

5. [HMWK]. Each student records all twelve sentences his or her group wrote and turns the tape in with the script (**#17 *Wish* and *Hope* Notes and Practice).**

6. Divide the class into pairs for an extended activity (using **#18 Modals + *Wish*/*Hope* Dialogue**) that will reinforce the use of *wish/hope,* review the use of modals, and provide content for introducing the articles *a/an/the.* As far as possible, ask students to pair themselves based on a common situation (work, school, etc.) or interests. Each pair agrees on a situation about which they will write a dialogue (maximum two minutes). Remind them that the intent is to practice and review modals and *wish/hope.*

Almost invariably, they will come up with more relevant situations than you can provide, but if necessary, here are some suggestions:

- renting an apartment
- a job interview
- a conversation between an advisor and a student
- opening a bank account
- making an appointment over the phone (haircut, dentist, etc.)
- asking for a date
- returning defective merchandise

Give pairs time to draft their dialogues and write them on #**18**. Circle the modals, underline wish/hope, and enter article phrases in the column on the right. As they finish, one pair can review and correct another pair's dialogue. Collect #**18** and keep it for review and revision after lesson 6, which covers the articles. Defer discussion of article usage in dialogues until then.

#16 What to Do with *Wish* and *Hope*

Wish is used to describe an unreal condition, i.e., to talk about something that cannot or most likely will not happen.

How to use *wish*	When to use *wish*	Additional examples
wish + past	Present [not true now] I wish I knew many languages. I wish I had a new car. I wish I were at the beach. I wish I knew.	
wish + *that** + past	I wish that you were here.	
wish + past progressive	I wish I were going with you. I wish they were moving out.	
wish + *could* or *wish* + *that** + *could*	Present [not possible now] I wish I could help. I wish I could go with you.	
wish + past perfect	Past [not true then] I wish I had known. I wish I had bought a car. I wish I had been smarter. I wish I had gone to the beach.	
wish + *that* + past perfect	I wish that it hadn't happened.	
wish + *could have* + past participle	Past [not possible then] I wish I could have helped.	
wish + *would* + verb	Future I wish you would listen to me. I wish you'd finish your work.	
wish + *that** + *would* + verb	I wish that you would cancel class. [*wish* used as a request is explained on #17.]	

Hope is used to describe a real condition; i.e., to talk about something that can or is likely to happen.

How to use *hope*	When to use *hope*	Additional examples
hope + present progressive	Present [possible now] I hope you're having fun.	
hope + present perfect *hope* + past *hope* + *that** + past progressive	Past [possible] I hope they've finished the work. I hope you didn't spend too much. I hope that you weren't waiting long.	
hope + present *hope* + future	Future [possible] I hope I win the lottery. I hope I'll see you in class.	

* The word *that* is used to introduce the clause. It is optional; the sentences may be spoken or written without it.

#17 *Wish* and *Hope* Notes and Practice

We use *wish* and *hope* to talk about something we want or would like. To put it as simply as possible, we use *wish* when we really **don't** expect that it will happen, and *hope* when we **do** expect that it will.

Wish   Transliteration = W2Sh
Notes
A wish [unreal] can also be expressed by using *if only* [2F10NL1].
I *wish* you were here. / *If only* you were here.
I *wish* you had listened to me. / *If only* you had listened to me.
The question of *were* versus *was*: Although in informal spoken English *was* is sometimes substituted for *were*, it is best to use *were* after the first and third person singular.
I wish I was/were at the beach. I wish she/he was/were here.
Wish + *would* used as a request refers to the present or future.
I wish she would stop that.

Hope   Transliteration = H10P
Notes
If the subject of the *hope* clause and the second clause are the same, there are three possible options:
hope + *to*   I hope to get a job soon.
hope + *that*   I hope that I can get a job soon. *hope* + *clause*   I hope I (will) get a job soon.
If the subject of the *hope* clause is different from the second clause, there are two possible options:
hope + *clause*   I hope he can get a job soon.
hope + *that*   I hope that he gets/will get a job soon.

Tense	Wish	Hope	Practice sentences
present	—	possible now/future	
future	—	possible future	
present progressive	—	possible now	
present perfect	—	possible past	
past progressive	not true now	possible past	
past	not true now	possible past	
could	not possible now	—	
past perfect	not true past	—	
could have	not possible past	—	
would	request/wish future (now)	—	

#18 Modals + *Wish*/*Hope* Dialogue

Pick a partner and create a dialogue that features the modals and a real or
unreal condition using *hope* and *wish*. After you have written your dialogue
in the column, circle the modals and the *wish/hope* words you've used.
Then, use the column marked Articles to list all the *a/an/the* phrases that
you used.

Script	Articles

Speaker _____ Partner _____

Lesson Six

Articles

1. Turn to the unnumbered sheet on *A, An,* and *The* and discuss it with the class (incorporating the information from FYI, above).

2. First, discuss pronunciation. Turn to charts **#19 Using *A/An*** and **#20 Using The.** After reviewing the pronunciation rules, practice with the sentences, asking students to fill in the appropriate pronunciation. Alternate responses on **#20** are acceptable if they can be defended. For example, in sentence 5, "This could be Th16 solution," or "This could be Th1 solution," are both possible.

3. There are several options for activities with sentences 7–10 on both **#19 Using *A/An*** and **#20 Using *The***:

   • Tape recording and transcription can be done as described on the charts.

- Students can work in pairs: student A says a sentence, student B writes it down verbatim. Student A then transliterates it.
- Assign the tape recording as homework. In this case, students will turn in **#19** and **#20** along with their tape.

4. Turn to **#21 Articles Pronunciation Guide.** Divide the class into three groups. Each group uses the pronunciation hints to diagram the articulation of one of the articles. Then each group leads the class in a final practice.

5. Next, go on to the grammar perspective. The confusion surrounding article usage can be greatly reduced by

- understanding the classification of English nouns as *countable* or *uncountable* and
- determining whether the context in which a noun is used is *general* or *specific.*

6. Begin with countability. Explain that in English every noun is classified as either countable or uncountable, based on whether or not it can be made plural. This classification is not always logical. For example, words like *team, child, tree,* and *leaf* have both a singular and a plural form and are therefore countable (e.g., *one leaf, five leaves*). On the other hand, nouns such as *information, advice, homework,* and *furniture* do not have a plural form and are therefore uncountable. However, the items that they represent can be made countable if they are preceded by a plural countable noun + *of,* as in

pieces of . . . furniture	*pages of . . . homework*
strands of . . . hair	*words of . . . advice*
cups of . . . coffee	*bags of . . . garbage*

7. Countability affects the use of both the verb and the article, i.e.,

- uncountable nouns are always singular and
- singular countable nouns must have an article or an equivalent determiner (e.g., *my* book, *whose* pen).

Ask the class to generate a short list of nouns and tell whether each is countable or uncountable. Add the uncountable nouns to **#22 Quick Reference: Some Common Uncountable Nouns.**

8. Discuss **#23 *A, An, The,* or No Article**. In part 1, stress that singular countable nouns must have an article (or a possessive modifier such as *my, his,* etc.). Tell the class that from now on, they should monitor for dropped articles. This will help them see how often the article is used and how often they themselves omit it. It will also take them from passive understanding and production in isolation toward correct usage in context.

A quick and effective way to help students when they omit articles is to ask, ''Is it countable?''

Student A:	I want to talk about my experience having Thanksgiving dinner in America.
Student B:	Was this the first time you experienced holiday in . . .
Teacher:	Wait . . . is *holiday* countable?
Student B:	Oh . . . **a** holiday. Was this the first time you experienced a holiday away from home?

Student:	Yesterday I go to gas station to put air in flat tire.
Teacher:	Can you count gas stations? Can you count air? Can you count tires?
Student:	Uh, one station, two stations . . . air . . . no . . . tires . . . yes.
Teacher:	So we need . . .
Student:	I go to **a** gas station to put air in **my** flat tire.
Teacher:	I went . . .
Student:	I went to a gas station to put air in my flat tire.

9. Continue with 2 on **#23 *A, An, The* or No Article**. Errors attributable to countability are common and lend themselves easily to a *yes/no* distinction. Furthermore, omitting an article where it is needed is clearly incorrect. Specificity, however, is often a matter of degree and open to interpretation. Errors in this category are more subtle, since substituting *the* for *a* or *an* or vice versa can change the intended meaning and result in miscommunication. For example, ''What did you buy?'' can be answered, ''I bought **the** book,'' or ''I bought **a** book,'' with an obvious difference in conveyed meaning. An effective way to help students work toward correct usage in this area is to ask, ''Is it general or specific?'' or ''Is it specific enough?''

10. The last two items on **#23 *A, An, The,* or No Article** are relatively straight-forward. Obvious or shared reference is self-explanatory. Article usage in

idiomatic expressions does not always follow the above rules. The phrases are invariable and must be learned as such.

11. **#24 No Article Situations** elaborates on some of the contexts in which no article is used. The sentences and phrases can also be used to practice linking. Section K can be assigned for transliteration and recording, with students contributing additional examples.

12. Refer students to **#25 Quick Reference: Which Article and Why.** Then turn to **#26 Articles Activity Sheet.** Working alone or in groups, students match the articles numbered in the passage with the corresponding rule in **#25.** (A teacher's answer key to **#26** is provided on **#26a.**) Students can work alone or in groups, identifying the rules for article use and practicing the phrases for linking and stress. Discuss correct answers as a class.

13. [HMWK]. The entire passage in **#26 Articles Activity Sheet** can be marked for linking, stress, and intonation and recorded, or just the phrases can be recorded.

14. Review Activity. The following activity consolidates concepts covered to this point. It can be used as a review in preparation for the integrative activity at the end of lesson 7.

    Return **#18 Modals +** *Wish/Hope* **Dialogue** from the end of lesson 5. Students work with their original partners to revise their dialogues, paying special attention to article usage. As pairs finish, students get in groups of four or six to correct each other's dialogues, focusing on grammar, vowel and consonant production, and linking. Pairs present their dialogues to the class.

A, An, and *The*

How important are the three little words that we call articles? How significant are they to comprehensibility? Small though they are, *a, an,* and *the* are powerful words in both pronunciation and grammar.

In speaking, the articles are most frequently pronounced as little noises which are linked to the following word. This linking created by the article is central to the stress and rhythm of a sentence. However, since the article is usually reduced, making it hard to hear, nonnative speakers often omit it completely, e.g., saying *I have book* instead of *I have a/the book.*

Learning to *speak* the articles requires constant attention. To avoid neglecting them, ask yourself, How many syllables does the sentence have? Tap them out. In *I have a book,* there are four. Now say the sentence slowly, emphasizing the linking to get used to including that little noise: 13H5V**16**B9K.

From the grammar perspective, learning to use *a, an,* and *the* is a troublesome task confounded by a clutter of rules and exceptions. We will focus on two major aspects of article usage. One is connected to the matter of the two English noun classes, *countables* and *uncountables.* The other aspect is related to deciding if something is *general* or *specific.*

#19 Using *A / An*

Pronunciation, not grammar or spelling, determines whether we use *a* or *an.*

Pronunciation

A precedes

- words beginning with consonant sounds,

  Vowel sound #16 is the most common pronunciation: There's *a* message for you.

  Vowel sound #3 is used only for special emphasis: I wanted *a* book, not all of them.

- words beginning with the letter *y,*

  a young man

- words that begin with the letter *u* when *u* is pronounced as a *y.*

  a uniform

An precedes all words that begin with vowel sounds,

  an orange

An is most frequently pronounced with vowel sound 16.

  [Note: The *n* is linked to the word following it. E.g., *16*N5PL.]

An is pronounced with vowel sound 5 in an isolated phrase or for special emphasis.

  5N apple
  5N11N16ST politician

In American English *an* precedes words beginning with the letter *h* when the *h* is not pronounced.

  hour, honor, honest, herb

Some speakers also use *an* before *hotel* and *historical,* but not before *history.*

Practice

First, fill in the blanks with the appropriate pronunciation of the underlined phrase, then record the sentences.

E.g., I want <u>an exact</u> *16N4GZ5KT* figure.

1. It might be <u>an excellent</u> _____ idea.

2. That certainly was <u>an odd</u> _____ situation.

3. We stayed in <u>an out of the way</u> _____ hotel.

4. They had become <u>a unified</u> _____ group.

5. This could be <u>a</u> _____ solution to our problem.

6. It's <u>an honor</u> _____ to meet you.

Now tape four of your own sentences. After you have recorded them, listen and then transcribe them in the space below. Do *not* write your sentences before you record them. Please follow this sequence because it will help you find out if you said the article and if you linked it to the next word.

7.

8.

9.

10.

#20 Using *The*

Pronunciation

The is pronounced with a voiced *Th* +

- vowel sound 16 when it comes before words beginning with consonants,

  Th16 bus stop
  Th16 first door on Th16 right

- vowel sound 1 when it comes before words beginning with vowel sounds,

  Th1 only way to go
  Th1 apartment on Th1 eleventh floor

- vowel sound 1 in front of words that begin with a *silent h,*

  herbs, honor, hour, honesty

- vowel sound 1 to emphasize or to indicate something special,

  Is that Th1 Dr. Livingstone?

- to indicate intensity or the superlative degree.

  That was Th1 worst exam I've ever taken.

Practice

First, fill in the blanks with the appropriate pronunciation of *the,* then record the sentences.

E.g., I just saw Th1 most wonderful movie.

1. That's _____ second parking ticket I've gotten this week.

2. _____ thrill of victory; _____ agony of defeat.

3. Was that _____ only thing you could do?

4. This could be _____ solution to _____ problem.

5. On _____ other hand, it could be _____ wrong approach.

6. _____ honorable Judge Simpson will be presiding at _____ hearing.

Now tape four of your own sentences. After you have recorded them, listen and then transcribe them in the space below. Do *not* write your sentences before you record them. Please follow this sequence because it will help you find out if you said the article and if you linked it to the next word.

7.

8.

9.

10.

#21 Articles Pronunciation Guide

Here are some notes that will help you pronounce the articles in context. You can also add some diagrams. Space is provided for you to add your own notes, e.g., how to link.

Article	Hints
a	Stretch the mouth into a slight grin position.
	The tongue remains flat.
	It can be either 3 or 16.
an	Use the same grin position as in *a*.
	Lower the upper teeth onto the tongue.
	It can be either 5N or 16N.
the	The front of the tongue is slightly between the upper and the lower teeth.
	It can be either Th16 or Th1.

#22 Quick Reference: Some Common Uncountable Nouns

A–G	H–K	L–Q	R–U	V–Z
advice	hair	luggage	research	vocabulary
baggage	homework	mail	slang	work
clothing	information	merchandise	traffic	
equipment	jewelry	news	travel	
furniture	knowledge	politics	trouble	
garbage		property		

You can add your own words to the above columns or reclassify the words into categories that make them easier to remember, e.g., clothing, baggage/luggage, and travel.

#23 *A, An, The,* or No Article?

Ask yourself these questions to help decide whether to use or omit the article.

1. Is this noun countable?

   Uncountable nouns are always singular.

   They never use *a/an.*

   They use *the* when they are specific.
   Furniture is expensive.
   The furniture in that store is expensive.

   Countable nouns must have an article (or another modifier) in the singular.

   Use *a/an* if the noun is general, *the* if it is specific.
   A dog was barking at me.
   The dog across the street was barking at me.

   Countable nouns in the plural have *the* or no article.

   Use no article if the noun is general, *the* if it is specific.
   Dogs always bark at me.
   The dogs across the street always bark at me.

2. Is the noun general or specific? Look in question 1 for which article to use.
   Homework is due every Friday. (uncountable, general)
   I haven't done **the** homework for tomorrow. (uncountable, specific)
   I bought **a** new car yesterday. (countable, singular, general)
   Please let me drive **the** car you bought yesterday. (countable, singular, specific)
   I love to drive big cars. (countable, plural, general)
   The big cars over there belong to my neighbor. (countable, plural, specific)

3. Does the noun have an obvious reference? Is there only one instance of it, or do the listener and speaker both know what is meant? If so, use *the.*
   the earth, **the** sky, **the** ground, **the** moon
   I'm going to **the** store and to **the** bank.
   He's in **the** hospital.
   The leak is in **the** bathroom.

4. Is the expression idiomatic? If it is, the lack of an article or article usage is part of the idiom and cannot be changed. For example:
   The apple doesn't fall far from **the** tree.
   the tail wagging **the** dog
   once in **a** lifetime
   She's going to school. [She's a student.]
   There was a fire at **the** school. [the school building]
   She's in prison. [She's a prisoner.]
   He's at **the** prison. [the prison building]
   They went **by train**, not **by bus.**
   They left **at night**, not **in the** morning.
   I have a computer **at home**, but not **at work.**
   by air, by phone, at school, in church, etc.

#24 No Article Situations

No article before

A. gerunds and uncountable nouns
   Health is more important than wealth.
   I'm not thrilled about driving at night.
B. fields of study
   I'm studying psychology.
C. mass nouns even when modified
   We must have clean water to survive.
D. abstract nouns that represent ideas, attitudes, emotions, qualities, or actions
   Jealousy frequently destroys relationships.
E. time designations and names of days and holidays
   Ramadan and Yom Kippur start at sundown, but Christian holidays start at sunrise.
F. names of general meals
   Would you believe that Jason eats cold pizza for breakfast?
G. most streets, roads
   I'll meet you at State and Liberty.
H. locations that have a specific activity, e.g., schools, courts (but not the building itself)
   You'll have to go to court if you want to appeal your ticket.
   While I'm at work, the children are in school.
   Exception: In American English we say "in **the** hospital"
I. titles when they are linked with proper nouns
   Father Domino met with Rabbi Khan, President Park, Queen Mary, Judge Li, and Admiral Aziz.

No *a/an* before

J. uncountable nouns
   No thanks, I don't like peanut butter with ice cream.

No article after

kind of
  The best *kind of* dishwasher will do pots and pans.
type of
  A phillip's head is a special *type of* screwdriver.
sort of
  What *sort of* apartment are you looking for?
brand of
  I don't like that *brand of* cereal.
variety of
  There's a *variety of* books on that subject.
make of
  What *make of* car do you have?
nature of
  It's the *nature of* teenagers to be moody.
*name of**
  What's the *name of* your dog?

Exceptions:

Most of/many of/much of
  Most of **the** money was invested.
  Many of **the** coins were gold.
  Much of **the** time was wasted.

---

*Always followed by a pronoun or *the.*

#25 Quick Reference: Which Article and Why

	General	Specific
Uncountable	1. Ø	2. *the*
Countable		
Singular	3. *a/an*	4. *the*
Plural	5. Ø	6. *the*

Obvious/shared reference

7. *the*

Idiomatic usage

8. Ø

a/an

the

#26 Articles Activity Sheet

Transliterate your pronunciation of the numbered article phrases. Then match the numbered article phrases with the number of the rule in **#25 Quick Reference Chart** to explain why that particular article was used or why there was no article.

Have you ever had someone steal [1] a parking space from you? Well it, happened to me one time. It was just before my four o'clock dentist appointment, and I had been circling [2] the parking structure for at least twenty minutes, hoping that [3] a space would open up. My appointments are always in [4] the late afternoon and getting parking [5] downtown is next to impossible at that time of [6] the day. [7] A feeling of relief came over me as I spotted [8] a man walking toward one of [9] the cars. I pulled closer and waited patiently as he unlocked [10] the door, fastened his seat belt, and did [11] an unbelievable number of other things before starting [12] the engine. Just as I began to think that he would never leave, he started to move. I backed up [13] a little to give him[14] the room he needed to pull out. Then, just as he pulled away, [15] a car raced past me and swung into [16] the space. I honked my horn furiously, but [17] the man just ignored me. He got out, locked his door, and walked away without even [18] a glance in my direction. I shouted, but that didn't do [19] a bit of good. Eventually, I did find [20] parking, but needless to say, I was very late for my appointment.

Transliteration	Article	Rule #
	1. a parking space	
	2. the parking structure	
	3. a space	
	4. the late afternoon	
	5. downtown	
	6. the day	
	7. a feeling of	
	8. a man	
	9. the cars	
	10. the door	
	11. an unbelievable number	
	12. the engine	
	13. a little	
	14. the room	
	15. a car	
	16. the space	
	17. the man	
	18. a glance	
	19. a bit of good	
	20. parking	

#26a Articles Activity Answer Sheet

Phrases	Answers
1. a parking space	3 countable, singular, general
2. the parking structure	7 shared reference *or* 4 countable, singular, specific, i.e., *the structure I was in*
3. a space	3 countable, singular, general
4. the late afternoon	8 idiomatic usage (*in the morning, at night . . .*)
5. downtown	1 uncountable, general
6. the day	7 shared reference *or* 8 [note: that time of day (idiomatic usage) is also acceptable.]
7. a feeling of	3 countable, singular, general. It *is* specific—a feeling of relief—but not specific enough. **The** *feeling of relief* would mean there is only one way to feel relief, shared by everyone.
8. a man	3 countable, singular, general
9. the cars	6 countable, plural, specific (implicit: *the cars in that structure*)
10. the door	7 shared reference = *the door of the car in question.*
11. an unbelievable number	8 a number of = some
12. the engine	4 countable, singular, specific (*engine of the car*)
13. a little	8 idiomatic usage *or* 3 countable, singular, general
14. the room	2 uncountable, specific
15. a car	3 countable, singular, general
16. the space	4 countable, singular, specific (*the space I was waiting for*)
17. the man	4 countable, singular, specific (*this particular man*)
18. a glance	3 countable, singular, general
19. a bit of good	8 idiomatic *or* 3 countable, singular, general
20. parking	1 uncountable, general

Lesson Seven

Beyond the Articles

1. Go to **#27 Beyond the Articles.** (Refer to **#28 Beyond the Articles Pronunciation Guide** for pronunciation hints.) Ask students to add to the examples, transliterate them, and practice linking and intonation.

2. Go on to **#29 Much versus Many** and **#30 Some versus Any,** soliciting examples from the class. Note that *much* is generally used in negative statements and questions but not in affirmative statements:

   - Does Osaka have much rain?
   - Osaka doesn't have much rain.
     but
   - Osaka has a lot/great deal of rain. (*not* Osaka has much rain.)

#31 Quick Reference: Countables/Uncountables provides an overview of countable and uncountable modifiers.

3. **Integrative activity.**
   #32a Integrative Critique Form lists the concepts covered to this point and is suitable as a midterm evaluation or test. Each student has two copies; one for self-evaluation and one for teacher evaluation. The activity proceeds as follows:

   - Discuss the form with the class. Under A and B, students should list up to three vowel and consonant sounds that they want to have evaluated.
   - In class or as homework, students compose a one- to two-minute narrative, recounting a conversation or experience. They should also try to include instances of all items under C.
   - Students practice their narrative several times (remembering to attend to the items in D) and then record it.

71

- Then students listen to their own recording and assess their perform-ance on **#32a.** Encourage them to make specific comments as well as to circle the numbers (4 being the highest).
- Students turn in their tapes, their completed form **#32a,** and their blank **#32b Integrative Critique Form.**
- You will use the student's **#32b** to assess his or her performance as you listen to each tape. Under *Additional Comments* you can note where your assessment agrees with the student's (indicating suc-cessful self-monitoring) and where it does not (indicating areas that still need work).
- Return the tape, **32a, 32b,** and the script.

#27 Beyond the Articles

Beyond the articles we have just finished studying are a number of other words that are frequently used to quantify nouns. The following list classifies some of the most commonly used ones on the basis of countability.

Used with both countable and uncountable nouns

			Additional examples and transliterations
no	N1O	no beans, no tofu	
a lack of	16L5K16V	a lack of engines and fuel	
some/any	S6M/4N1	some/any chips and dip	
lots of	L7TZ16V	lots of fries and ketchup	
a lot of	16L7D16V	a lot of rocks and sand	
more	M7R	more biscuits and tea	
this	Th2S	this problem/jewelry	
that	Th5T	that book/furniture	
plenty of	PL4N1 - Y7V	plenty of desks and space	

Used only with countable nouns

			Additional examples and transliterations
these	Th1Z	these tickets	
those	Th1OZ	those companies	
several	S4VR16L	several courses	
a few	16FY8	a few chairs	
fewer	FY8W12	fewer problems	
many	M4N1	many languages	
a couple of	16K6P16L16V	a couple of spaces	

Used only with uncountable nouns

			Additional examples and transliterations
much	M6Ch	much work	
less	L4S	less trouble	
a little	16L2DL	a little trouble	

#28 Beyond the Articles Pronunciation Guide

	Hints
several	commonly reduced to two syllables, S4VRL or reduce middle vowel sound to S4V16RL
plenty of	pronounced as PL4N1[Y]16V formal pronunciation PL4NT1 (not a *flapped d*)
a lot of	link all three words, 16L7D16V link the phrase to the word that follows if that word begins with a vowel, e.g., *a lot of onions*
more	M7R stretch the vowel sound
less	L4S stretch the vowel sound
few/fewer	insert *y* between *f* and the vowel sound, FY8 insert *w* before the second syllable, FY8W12
a little	link the two words and use *flapped d,* 16L2DL
this/that	voiced Th + 2S/5T
these/those	voiced Th + 1Z/10Z

#29 *Much versus Many*

Much M6CH	Many M4N1
Much is used with uncountable nouns	*Many* is used with plural countable nouns
e.g.,	e.g.,
[Practice sentence and transliteration]	[Practice sentence and transliteration]
Phrases that can substitute for *much* a good/great deal of	Phrases that can substitute for *many* a good/great number of
e.g.,	e.g.,
[Practice sentence and transliteration]	[Practice sentence and transliteration]
a great/large quantity of	
e.g.,	
[Practice sentence and transliteration]	

Phrases that can substitute for much *and* many

a lot of/lots of

e.g., [Practice sentence and transliteration]

plenty of

e.g., [Practice sentence and transliteration]

#30 *Some* versus *Any*

Some S6M	Any 4N1
• indicates presence of a quantity or an amount	• indicates complete absence of a quantity
• used mostly in positive statements and questions	• used mostly in negative statements and questions
• used with singular count nouns to indicate a degree somewhere between general and specific	• used in positive statements and questions to mean *it doesn't matter which* or *any at all* You can take *any* seat.
• used to indicate something specific but unknown [often with the phrase *or other*] I put it *some* place [or other].	• used to indicate *no exception* *Any* junk mail that I get goes straight into the trash.
• used before a number to indicate approximation The paper said *some* 10,000 people showed up.	

Some or *any* used as substitutes for general plural nouns or noun phrases

I'd like to borrow *some* eggs. Sorry, I don't have *any* [eggs], but I'm going to the store and I can get you *some*.

[Practice sentences and transliteration]

1.

2.

3.

Some or *any* used with uncountables

I need *some* sugar, too. Sorry, I don't have *any* sugar either. Should I buy you *some* of that, too?

[Practice sentences and transliteration]

1.

2.

3.

#31 Quick Reference: Countables / Uncountables

Countables	Uncountables
a few	less
a number of	an amount/great deal of
fewer	how much
how many	much
many	a little
several	
these	
those	

Can be used with both

a lack of
a lot of
any
more
most
no
plenty of
some
this*
that*

---

*not used with plural countables

#32a Integrative Critique Form

Speaker: _____   Critic: _____

#____ e.g., _____   #____ e.g., _____

A. Vowel sounds

B. Consonant sounds

e.g., _____   e.g., _____

C. Modals	1	2	3	4	Comment
If- clauses	1	2	3	4	Comment
Wish/hope	1	2	3	4	Comment
A/an/the	1	2	3	4	Comment
D. Linking	1	2	3	4	Comment
Contractions	1	2	3	4	Comment
Stress	1	2	3	4	Comment

E. Additional comments

#32b Integrative Critique Form

Speaker: _____   Critic: _____

A. Vowel sounds

\# _____ e.g., _____   \# _____ e.g., _____

B. Consonant sounds

\# _____ e.g., _____   \# _____ e.g., _____

C.	Modals	1	2	3	4	Comment
	If- clauses	1	2	3	4	Comment
	Wish/hope	1	2	3	4	Comment
	A/an/the	1	2	3	4	Comment
D.	Linking	1	2	3	4	Comment
	Contractions	1	2	3	4	Comment
	Stress	1	2	3	4	Comment

E. Additional comments

Lesson Eight

Pronouns

1. Begin with **#33 Pronoun Activity Sheet.** Students read the paragraph to themselves, underlining all the names. Then, in small groups, students first decide which names will be male and which female. (These names have been chosen specifically because they can be either male or female.) The groups then substitute appropriate pronouns for the underlined proper nouns. When all have finished, each group compares its version with another group's and then with **#34 Sample Version** on the following page.

2. In pairs or small groups, mark phrasing and linking in **#34 Sample Version.** Discuss the exercise as a class, then practice it as a choral reading.

3. For additional practice with *he* and *she,* groups can practice their own versions and present them to the class as a group choral reading.

4. Discuss **#35 Pronoun Do's and Don'ts.** Let students add examples to the categories.

5. Go on to **#36 Pronouns.** Note that the class is already familiar with some of these, which also appeared in **#27 Beyond the Articles** (*some, any, much, many,* etc.). Add S, P, or B to each box on **#36** to indicate whether the pronoun takes a singular verb, a plural verb, or both. This can be done as a quiz or test, as a class discussion, in small groups, or as homework.

6. Ask students individually to write a brief narrative of an interaction, focusing on pronoun use. They might choose

    *   relating a piece of gossip from their own experience,
    *   explaining a short segment from a soap opera or other television show or movie, or
    *   being given a traffic ticket.

Use **#37 Pronoun Narrative.** This sheet is followed by charts for quick reference: **#38 Quick Reference: Singular or Plural** and **#39 Quick Reference: Possessive Pronouns/Reflexive Pronouns.**

7. In small groups, students listen to each other's narratives, correcting pronoun usage, linking, and phrasing.

8. [HMWK]. Students rewrite their corrected narrative on **#37a Revised Pronoun Narrative** and record it. They hand in the tape and **#37a,** which includes a teacher's critique form.

#33 Pronoun Activity Sheet

1. Read the following paragraph.
2. Underline the proper nouns.
3. In groups of three, decide which will be male and which will be female names.
4. Rewrite the paragraph, substituting appropriate pronouns.
5. Compare your group version with the sample version on the next page.

Terry told Sandy that Terry was surprised that Pat didn't get the homework done for the Chem Lab. Sandy told Terry that Sandy saw Lee do something that might explain why. Sandy said that Pat told Sandy that Lee asked Pat if Lee could borrow Pat's homework so Lee could check if Lee's answers were correct. The next morning before class when Pat asked Lee for Pat's homework, Lee told Pat that Lee had lost the homework. When the professor asked the students to turn in the students' homework, Sandy saw Lee erase Pat's name from the homework sheet and hand in Pat's homework as Lee's own work.

#34 Sample Version

The following is one possible rewrite. The substitutions are shown in italics.

Terry — male
Sandy — male
Pat — female
Lee — female

Terry told Sandy that *he* was surprised that Pat didn't get the homework done for the Chem Lab. Sandy said *he* saw Lee do something that might explain why. *He* said that Pat told *him* that Lee had asked *her* if she could borrow *her* homework to check if *her* answers were correct. The next morning before class when Pat asked Lee for *her* homework, Lee told *her she* couldn't find *it*. When the professor asked the students to turn in *their* homework, Sandy saw Lee erase Pat's name from the homework sheet and hand *it* in as *her* own.

#35 Pronoun Do's and Don'ts

Do	Don't

1. Make sure the pronoun agrees in *number* with its *antecedent* (the word or words the pronoun refers to).

   Pronoun *quantifiers* such as *all, a lot, some, no,* and *none* are especially problematic because they take a singular verb with uncountable nouns and a plural verb with countable plural nouns.

   Is sand white?
   Some *is*.

   Are beaches white?
   Some *are.*

   Additional examples:

1. Don't let adjectives or phrases confuse you. A singular subject takes a singular verb.

   incorrect: The answer to all these questions *are* very difficult to find.
   correct: The answer to all these questions *is* very difficult to find.

2. Make sure the pronoun agrees with its antecedent in *gender*;

   he, him, his, himself = masculine singular
   she, her, hers, herself = feminine singular

   Use *his or her* to make a statement about a group that includes both males and females. (*Their* is frequently used in informal spoken English.)

   Additional examples:

2. Don't use the masculine singular to represent a generalized member of a group that has males and females.

   incorrect: Everyone should do *his* own work.
   correct: Everyone should do *his or her* own work.

Do	Don't
3. Make sure that the antecedent (referent) of the pronoun is obvious and without ambiguity. She told her brother that he had to do the dishes. Additional examples:	3. Don't use a pronoun to refer to something that is vague or ambiguous. incorrect: She told her sister that *she* had to do the dishes. correct: She told her sister to do the dishes. correct: She told her sister that she would do the dishes herself.
4. Remember that prepositions such as *between, for,* and *to* take the objective case so the grammatically correct pronouns that follow are objective case pronouns. it's between *him/her/them* and *me/us.* Jorge sent those for Tau and *me.* Additional examples:	4. Don't use the subjective case pronoun *I* after prepositions, even though you hear native speakers use it. incorrect: The flowers were *for* Junko and *I.* It's all over *between* John and *I.* correct: The flowers were *for* Junko and *me.* It's all over *between* John and *me.*
5. Remember that the possessive pronouns are written without an apostrophe, i.e., *ours, yours, his, hers, its,* and *theirs.* This is *yours,* not *theirs.* Additional examples:	5. Don't write the possessive pronouns with an apostrophe. (The apostrophe signals a contraction.) incorrect: Is this book *your's*? correct: Is this book *yours*?

#36 Pronouns

The usual listing of pronouns is as follows:

Singular				Plural			
Subjective	*Objective*	*Possessive* *	*Reflexive*	*Subjective*	*Objective*	*Possessive*	*Reflexive*
I	me	mine	myself	we	us	ours	ourselves
you	you	yours	yourself	you	you	yours	yourselves
he, she, it	him, her, it	his, hers, its	himself, herself, itself	they	them	theirs	themselves
who/one	whom/—	whose/ one's	oneself	who	whom	whose	

* *My, your, our, and their* are also possessive, but they are adjectives.

The following are some other words that frequently function as pronouns. Use the letters **S**, **P**, and **B** to indicate whether they take a **S**ingular verb, a **P**lural verb, or **B**oth.

_____ all
_____ another
_____ any
_____ anybody
_____ anyone
_____ anything
_____ both
_____ each (one)
_____ either
_____ enough
_____ every
_____ everybody
_____ everyone
_____ everything
_____ few
_____ fewer
_____ half
_____ kind
_____ least

_____ less
_____ little
_____ many
_____ more
_____ most
_____ much
_____ neither
_____ no
_____ no one
_____ nobody
_____ none
_____ nothing
_____ one, two, etc.
_____ other(s)
_____ person
_____ plenty
_____ several
_____ some
_____ somebody

_____ someone
_____ something
_____ sort
_____ that
_____ these
_____ this
_____ those
_____ type
_____ what
_____ whatever
_____ whatsoever
_____ which
_____ whichever
_____ whoever
_____ whole
_____ whomever
_____ whosoever

#37 Pronoun Narrative

1. Review #35 and #36.
2. Write a short narrative (maximum recording time two minutes). See suggested topics below.
3. Present your narrative to your group for corrections.
4. Edit your script, then rewrite it on #37a.
5. Underline the pronouns, indicate your phrasing. Mark linking and vowel sound numbers for the articles.
6. Record the script from #37a.
7. Hand in your tape and the #37a script.

Suggested topics: Relating a piece of gossip from your own experience, explaining a short segment from a soap opera, or describing what happened when you got a traffic ticket.

Rough draft

Cast of characters/Who's talking to whom

1. _____   2. _____   3. _____

#37a Revised Pronoun Narrative

Name _____ Date _____

Edited script

Cast of characters/Who's talking to whom

1. _____   2. _____   3. _____

Teacher's critique

	Rating				Comments
Pronoun use	1	2	3	4	
Phrasing	1	2	3	4	
Linking	1	2	3	4	
Vowel sounds	1	2	3	4	

In addition, review lesson(s) / chart(s)

Overall rating   1   2   3   4

#38 Quick Reference: Singular or Plural

Singular or plural depending on the words they represent

e.g., *all* gold *is* expensive / *all* diamonds *are* expensive.

all

any

half

more

most

some

Singular pronouns and endings   **Plural**

one   both

each   few

either   many

neither   several

-one

-body

-thing

#39 Quick Reference: Possessive Pronouns /
Reflexive Pronouns

Possessive Pronouns

Pronoun + noun	Pronoun (no noun)
my book	mine
your book	yours
his book	his
her book	hers
its book	its
our book	ours
their book	theirs

Reflexive Pronouns

Used only when the object refers to the subject.

Singular	Plural
myself	ourselves
yourself	yourselves
himself*	themselves*
herself	
itself	

---

* Although you may sometimes hear native speakers use *hisself* and *theirselves*, these forms are not considered standard English.

Lesson Nine

Two-Word Combinations

1. This lesson deals with three types of two-word combinations that frequently present problems of stress placement and linking:

   - verb + preposition
   - noun + noun
   - adjective + noun

2. Start with the verb + preposition combination: ask students to generate five to ten examples. Then discuss the following points about these combinations, often referred to as two-word or phrasal verbs:

   - They have a specific meaning as a unit, not the meaning of the verb plus the meaning of the preposition (e.g., *look up* means to research, as opposed to raising the eyes; *look under*, on the other hand, never has a separate meaning as a unit).
   - They can be classified into two subgroups: *separable* and *inseparable*.
   - In the separable group, the verb and preposition can be separated by a noun, e.g., *hand in* an assignment, *hand* an assignment *in.* The verb and preposition must be separated if there is a pronoun (*hand it in*). In this group, stress is on the preposition, not the verb.*
   - In the inseparable group, the verb and preposition are never separated (*run into* John, *run into* him; *hit on* a solution, *hit on* it). In this group, phrase stress does not follow any rule. Since stress placement is unpredictable, it must be learned with the phrase.

   In addition, there are a number of common three-word verbs that also have a specific unit meaning, such as *look in on* (visit with the purpose of checking), *stand up for* (to back or support), or *put up with* (tolerate). In

---

*When these combinations are used as nouns, the stress shifts from the preposition to the noun, e.g., *work out* versus a *workout*, *push over* versus a *pushover*.

these phrases the first and second words cannot be separated, but an adverb can be inserted between the second and third words:

- The doctor looked in *regularly* on the patient.
- The doctor *regularly* looked in on the patient.
- The doctor looked in on the patient *regularly*.

In these combinations, phrase stress is on the first preposition (look __ put __

Phrasal verbs are extremely common, especially in oral communication. Often they have single-word synonyms frequently found in writing and other more formal circumstances (e.g., *blow up/explode*; *check out/investigate*).

3. Turn to activity sheet **#40 Two-Word Combinations 1**. Review the examples generated earlier. As a class, enter those that are true phrasal verbs in the appropriate columns. Then, in small groups, students add as many others as they can think of. For each, they determine whether it is a true phrasal verb or a verb plus preposition(s) and discuss its meaning.

4. Following this discussion, use the same activity sheet (**#40 Two-Word Combinations 1**) to focus on the separable/inseparable aspect. Explain that there is no logic to whether a phrasal verb is separable or inseparable; a verb is either one or the other and must be learned that way. Then

- Assign each small group two or three columns on the activity sheet. The group labels each verb as *S* for separable or *I* for inseparable.
- Each group chooses five of the verbs from its columns and creates sentences.
- The group practices the sentences, focusing on stress and linking.
- Each group teaches the class its sentences, focusing on how to pronounce and use the verbs.

5. [HMWK]. Students begin collecting phrasal verbs that they hear frequently in their daily environment (work, school, shopping, etc.), entering them on **#41 Phrasal Verbs Journal**. Students should continue to make entries throughout the course. Journal entries can be used at any time by having students briefly (one minute) explain and teach one of their entries to the class.*

---

*Phrasal verb collections usually contain many slang expressions. Explaining their meanings provides an easy and uncontrived way to include discussions around the cultural values they convey.

6. In pairs or groups of three, students write a short dialogue or conversation using some of the entries from their journals (**#41 Phrasal Verbs Journal**). Students may use the following examples as models for their own dialogues or conversations.

    Dialogue

    A: I just learned a new two-word verb.
    B: Oh really, which one?
    A: *Go into.*
    B: Going to?
    A: No, *go into*.
    B: Do you mean like *go into a room*?
    A: No, it's like *talk about in detail*.
    B: Oh, where did you hear that?
    A: I'd rather not *go into* that.

    Conversation

    A: Hi, what's up?
    B: Fernando and I are trying to *make up* this dialogue for our English class.
    C: Yeah, and it has to be *turned in* tomorrow.
    A: Why do you have to *turn it in*?
    B: Well, the teacher wants to *look it over*.
    C: She's going to *go over it* for us to make sure we haven't *messed up*.
    A: Well, are you almost done so we can *go out* to dinner?
    B: Almost; we just want to *look up* a couple of words.
    C: We shouldn't have *put it off* till the last minute, but I think we'd better finish it before we go.

    Selected dialogues can be presented to the class and critiqued by the entire class or a few class members on **#42 Phrasal Verbs Critique Form**. All should be handed in for correction. Although the first group to present will have the disadvantage of not having heard previous critiques, this can be overcome by offering only that group a second chance to present a revised version at the end of all the presentations.

7. Go on to **#43 Two-Word Combinations 2: Phrasal Nouns**. These are noun + noun or adjective + noun combinations that work in the same way as verb + preposition in that they create a specific unit meaning. In this case,

the stress is always on the first word of the pair, since stress on the second word makes it a normal adjective + noun combination where the adjective modifies the noun (e.g., the *Yellow* Pages is a specific directory of suppliers and services supplied by the telephone company, as opposed to *yellow pages*, which are yellow pieces of paper).

8. Practice the expressions on **#43 Two-Word Combinations 2: Phrasal Nouns** for stress. Then ask students to create sentences using some of the examples, indicating stress, linking, and phrasing. Have students generate additional examples and critique informally.

9. Go on to **#44 Two-Word Combinations 3.** These are noun + noun combinations* in which the first word functions as an adjective and receives the stress. These combinations are extremely common in English (a list of examples appears as **#44a Two-Word Combinations 3: More Examples**) and new ones appear routinely (e.g., *laser disc, sound bite*). The meaning is generally something like "noun 2 for/of noun 1," i.e., *driver for cab, dressing for salad, ache of a tooth, plane for the air*. When students question whether a given expression belongs to this group, they can double check by putting it into the x of y format. If it works, stress the first noun:

   • Is a refrigerator magnet a magnet for the refrigerator?
   • Yes, so stress *refrigerator*.

   Stress is on the second word only to correct a miscommunication or for special emphasis, e.g., "I need brake pads, but not brake shoes."

10. Students should have no trouble generating many examples to add to the list. As in the previous activity, they can then create practice sentences to present to the class or in small groups. Drill and repeat these combinations, along with the phrasal verbs from **#40 Two-Word Combinations 1** and the phrasal nouns from **#43 Two-Word Combinations 2: Phrasal Nouns** to help students internalize this stress pattern.

---

*Or sometimes participle + noun as in *sleeping bag, bowling ball*. The participle + noun combination can also be placed in the phrasal noun category.

#40 Two-Word Combinations 1

Verbs + Prepositions

In each column list verbs that are combined with the preposition to create a phrasal verb. Your entries must include pronunciation information: vowel sound numbers, stress, linking, reductions, and deletions.

up	down	in	out	on	off	over	with	others
		hand in H5ND2N			put off P9T7F			across about ahead around away between by for into through under without

#41 Phrasal Verbs Journal

List commonly heard verb phrases, define the unit meaning, indicate whether the phrase is separable [S] or inseparable [I], then use it in a sentence. In the last column, transliterate the phrasal verb and indicate the stress.

Verb phrase	Unit meaning	S/I	Practice sentence	Transliteration

#42 Phrasal Verbs Critique Form

Speaker _____ Date _____

Phrasal verb(s)

Meaning

Meaning clear?   Yes   No
Comment

Separable?   Yes   No
Comment

Modals   1   2   3   4
Examples

Articles   1   2   3   4
Examples

Phrase stress   1   2   3   4
Examples

Linking   1   2   3   4
Examples

Consonant sounds requiring attention

_____ as in _____

_____ as in _____

_____ as in _____

Vowel sounds requiring attention

_____ as in _____

_____ as in _____

_____ as in _____

Additional comments

Critic _____ Date _____

#43 Two-Word Combinations 2: Phrasal Nouns

Phrasal nouns are a **noun + noun** or (frequently) an **adjective + noun** that create a specific unit meaning analogous to phrasal verbs. The stress is on the **first** word. (Stress on the second word makes it a noun modified by an adjective.) E.g., a **short**stop is the term for a specific player on a baseball team whereas a short **stop** is a brief pause.

Examples

shortstop	candybar
coldcream/cuts	country club
running coach	White House
darkroom	mouthpiece
wall/head/backboard	greenhouse
hotdog	pigskin
skinhead	gridiron
yellowjacket	raincheck

Practice Sentences

Indicate stress, vowel sound numbers, linking, and phrasing.

1.

2.

3.

4.

5.

6.

7.

#44 Two-Word Combinations 3

Usually **noun** + **noun.** The stress is on the first word. The first noun functions as an adjective. The meaning of the two together can be shown as noun 2 of / for noun 1, e.g., babysitter = sitter of / for babies.

Stress on the second word is only to correct miscommunication or for special emphasis, e.g., ''I wanted more salad **dressing,** not another salad **bowl.**''

Examples

book-/shopkeeper	day/night/gearshift
dog/cat/baby/healthfood	repair/dress/barbershop
washing/stamping machine	clothing/shoe/furniture store
blow/hair/clothes dryer	slide/movie projector
toaster/wall oven	public health/policy
drive/pass through	water/wind damage
bloodcount/pressure	news-/term/typing paper
head-/stomach-/ear-/backache	parking stucture/lot
lab/blood tests	planning/drain commission
game theory/show	air-conditioning/-plane/-port
key-/poster/diving board	tax break/return/shelter
color/hall monitor	meat/soup/dog bone
cross-check/-reference	pain-/serial killer
light bulb/show/meter	bank loan/deposit
golf course/club/ball	hairstyle/-cut
ground-/distilled/well water	surface tension/missile

Practice Sentences

Indicate stress, vowel sound numbers, linking, phrasing.

1.

2.

3.

4.

5.

6.

7.

8.

#44a Two-Word Combinations 3: More Examples

Add your own to the list below.

art gallery	physics department
babysitter	police officer
cabdriver	raincoat
carwash	salad dressing
coffee grinder	science teacher
computer science	sit com
convenience store	soap opera
crossing guard	tap dancing
fighter pilot	teapot
firefighter	toothache
health care	walk-up/drive-up window
insurance policy	video store
landfill	hot plate*
laser printer	softball*
mailbox	supermarket*
military action	

---

* Occasionally, adjective + noun combinations also have this pattern.

Lesson Ten

Words with Stress Change

1. The focus now shifts from words that *combine* to words that *change.* This is a group of words that change stress depending on whether they are used as nouns (stressed on the first syllable) or verbs (stressed on the second syllable). The spelling does not change.

2. Turn to **#45 Noun or Verb**. Group students in pairs or threes. Each group transliterates all the words on the list. Then each group creates sentences for three or four of the words. After practicing their sentences, groups teach the rest of the class by writing their sentences on the board. They discuss stress, linking, and phrasing and lead the class in a choral reading.

3. The second page of **#45 Noun or Verb** covers some of the common exceptions to the stress rules practiced above. Practice activities on this chart can be discussed as a class.

4. Go on to **#46 Noun/Adjective or Verb**. These words, all ending in *-ate*, do not change stress, but do change the vowel sound, depending on usage. Practice the examples and ask students if they know others; then create sentences. Small groups can teach the class in the same manner as in **#45 Noun or Verb**.

5. Students individually write a short piece (narrative, explanation, etc.) using the various types of two-word combinations. The piece can be something of interest to the entire class (recipe, how-to talk, etc.) or something very specific to the individual (work situation, etc). Students use **#47 Looking for Word Combinations** to prepare the script and list all combinations. The teacher can move around the room giving help.

6. Narratives can be presented as follows:

- Before presenting, the speaker writes the word combinations from his or her passage on the board.
- Class members (or a few class members) copy the word combinations onto **#48 Word Combinations Critique.**
- During the presentation, critics listen for vowel sounds and phrase stress of the word combinations, noting errors on **#48.**
- The presenter receives all the **#48** sheets.

These presentations should be staggered over a period of several sessions, i.e., do not have all the presentations on one day.

7. To extend this activity to include a teacher critique, after presenting and receiving critique forms, students can record and transcribe a corrected monologue and turn them in for a critique.

8. An alternative is to forego the presentations in class and ask students to record their monologues at home. They then hand in the scripts and tapes for teacher critique.

#45 Noun or Verb

There are a number of words in English that can be used both as nouns and verbs. Although the two forms are spelled the same, the word stress is different: The *noun* form is stressed on the first syllable. The *verb* form is stressed on the second syllable.* These words generally have prefixes. This noun form stress is unusual, since prefixes are usually not stressed in English.

Noun/verb	Transliteration + stress		Practice Sentences
			Indicate stress, vowel sound numbers, linking, phrasing.
affect	5F4KT	16F4KT	
defect			
object			
project			
reject			
subject			
suspect			
present			
converse			
convert			
contrast			
conduct			
discharge			
permit			
progress			
produce			
record			
survey			

---

* Some exceptions are listed on the next page of this chart.

Words where the stress does **not** change or changes in a special way.

Noun/verb	Transliteration + stress	Practice sentences
comment	K7M4NT	[as a **noun**]
		[as a **verb**]
effect		[as a **noun**]
		[as a **verb**]
reverse		[as a **noun**]
		[as a **verb**]
		[as a **noun**]
		[as a **verb**]
		[as a **noun**]
		[as a **verb**]

The word *address:* 1. When it is stressed on the first syllable [5DR4S], it can only be a noun.

                2. When it is stressed on the second syllable [16DR4S], it can be used as a noun or a verb.

Practice sentences using *address:*

[5DR4S]   1.

[16DR4S]   2.

           3.

The word *desert:* 1. The word *desert* [D4Z12T] is the noun/adjective meaning a dry, barren region.

                2. The word *desert* [D16Z12T] is the noun meaning what one deserves and is usually plural.

                3. The word *desert* [D16Z12T] is the verb meaning to abandon something or someone.

Note: The word D16Z12T, spelled with a double *s* (*dessert*), is what you eat after your main meal; usually some sweet food, fruit, cheese, etc.

Practice sentence using *desert:*

[D4Z12T]   1.

[D16Z12T] 2.

[D16Z12T] 3.

#46 Noun / Adjective or Verb

These words can be used as adjectives, nouns, or verbs. Depending on usage, the vowel sound changes:

- as a noun/adjective, the -ate syllable at the end is pronounced 16T
- as a verb, it is pronounced 3T

Note that the stress does not change.

Noun/adjective	Verb
advocate [5DV16K16T]	[5DV16K3T]
separate [S4P12R16T]	[S4P12R3T]
moderate [M7D12R16T]	[M7D12R3T]
elaborate [16L5B12R16T]	[1L5B12R3T]
estimate [4ST16M16T]	[4ST16M3T]
degenerate [D1J4N12R16T]	[D1J4N12R3T]
delegate [D4L16G16T]	[D4L16G3T]
approximate [16PR7KS16M16T]	[16PR7KS16M3T]

Practice sentences

Indicate stress, vowel sound numbers, linking, and phrasing.

1.
2.
3.
4.
5.
6.
7.
8.
9.
10.

#47 Looking for Word Combinations

Instructions: Write your script below. Circle any word combinations you've used, e.g., verb + preposition, compound noun, etc. Then list them in the Word combinations column.

Speaker   **Word combinations**

_____

_____

_____

_____

_____

_____

_____

_____

_____

_____

_____

_____

_____

_____

_____

_____

_____

_____

_____

_____

_____

_____

_____

#48 Word Combinations Critique

Instructions for critiques:

List the speaker's word combinations.
Enter vowel sound number and phrase stress errors.

Speaker _____ Date _____

Word combination	Vowel sounds	Phrase stress
_____	_____	_____
_____	_____	_____
_____	_____	_____
_____	_____	_____
_____	_____	_____
_____	_____	_____
_____	_____	_____
_____	_____	_____
_____	_____	_____

Additional comments

Critic _____ Date _____

Lesson Eleven

Endings with Pronunciation Changes

FYI

The pronunciation of the past tense *-ed* ending is determined by the voiced/voiceless distinction. Sounds that are voiced produce vocal cord vibration; voiceless sounds do not. All vowel sounds are voiced; consonant sounds are either voiced or voiceless as shown in **#2 Consonant Sound Categories.**

Specifically:

1. Verbs that end in the voiceless sounds *p, k, ch, s, sh, f,* and *θ* cause the past tense *-ed* to become voiceless also, so it is pronounced *-t* (as in *jumped, asked, watched, missed, wished,* and *laughed*).

2. Verbs that end in voiced sounds *b, g, dӡ, z, v, Th, m, ŋ, l,* and *r* and in vowels cause the past tense *-ed* to become voiced also, so it is pronounced *-d* (as in *robbed, begged, hedged, pleased, loved, breathed, blamed, hanged, pulled, poured, earned, played, eyed, oohed,* and *aahed*).

3. Only in verbs that end in *-t* or *-d* is the past tense *-ed* pronounced as an extra syllable (*wanted, crowded, needed,* and *rented*).

When these forms are used as adjectives or nouns, the *-ed* ending becomes an extra syllable pronounced -16D. For example, *a learned* (L12N16D) *scholar, the wicked* (W2K16D) *witch, the blessed* (BL4S16D), *the aged* (3J16D).

These distinctions should be explained to the class *after* students have completed their work on **#49 The Past Tense: *-ed*** and attempted to formulate rules themselves.

---

1. Elicit from the class examples of *regular* past tense verb forms (e.g., *jumped, produced, pretended, wanted, learned*). Write them on the board; do not correct pronunciation yet.

2. Use **#49 The Past Tense: -ed** to introduce the three pronunciations of this ending. Divide the class into small groups. Each group finds as many past tense examples as possible and enters them in one of the three boxes on the chart. Start with the examples collected above. When there are at least ten entries in each box, the group formulates pronunciation rules and diagrams the articulation of the three past tense sounds.

3. Each group writes the rules it has formulated on the board. Use the explanations in **FYI,** page 113, to correct the students' rules. Have groups correct their own examples by testing them against the rules.

4. [HMWK]. Ask students to record their examples on tape. To correct the tape, model only the mispronounced words. Ask the student to practice and re-record those words in isolation and in a sentence.

5. Each student chooses three verbs from the boxes on **#49 The Past Tense: -ed,** creates a past tense sentence with each, and enters them on **#50 Hearing the Past.**

6. Now, divide the class into groups of five to ten students. Members of the group take turns reading their sentences. The other group members take notes on what they hear and report back to the speaker. The speaker records whether his or her past tense forms were correct, and if not, what requires further practice.

7. For additional practice, students can be asked to categorize and record the verbs in **#51 Back to the Past.**

8. Following the same format as in the *-ed* exercise, elicit from the class examples of words ending in *-s* and write them on the board (e.g., *peas, leaves, halves, misses, watches, wishes, thoughts, thinks, asks, takes, studies, plays, fields, tires, shots, judges*).

FYI

The pronunciation of the *-s* ending is also determined by the voiced/voiceless distinction. Sounds that are voiced produce vocal cord vibration; voiceless sounds do not. All vowel sounds are voiced; consonant sounds are either voiced or voiceless as shown in **#2 Consonant Sound Categories.**

Specifically:

1. Words that end in the voiceless sounds *p, t, k, f,* and *θ* cause the *-s* to become voiceless also, so it is pronounced *-s* (as in *jumps, payments, mosques, asks, laughs,* and *breaths*).

2. Words that end in the voiced sounds *b, d, g, v, Th, m, n, ŋ, l,* and *r* and in vowels cause the *-s* to become voiced also, so it is pronounced *-z* (as in *robs, crowds, pigs, leaves, blames, learns, breathes, earnings, stumbles, pours, plays, eyes, oohs,* and *aahs*).

3. In words that end in the sounds *s, z, ch, sh, ʤ,* and *x** the ending becomes *-es,* an extra syllable that is pronounced *-ez* (*buses, loses, churches, wishes, edges, garages,* and *boxes*).

These distinctions can be explained to the class after students have completed their work on **#52 The *-s* Ending: Third Person Singular/Noun Plural** and attempted to formulate rules themselves.

---

9. Use **#52 The *-s* Ending: Third Person Singular/Noun Plural** to introduce the three pronunciations of this ending. Divide the class into small groups. Each group finds as many *-s* examples as possible and enters them in one of the three boxes on the chart. Start with the examples collected above. When there are at least ten entries in each box, the group formulates pronunciation rules and diagrams the articulation of the three *-s* ending sounds.

---

*The ʤ sound is spelled *-dge* or *-ge* as in *judge, badge, footage,* etc. The ʒ sound is spelled *-ge* as in *garages.* This sound is rarely found at the end of words in English (*corsage, collage*). It does occur with some frequency in the middle (e.g., *measure, pleasure, television, decision*). The letter *x* is pronounced *-ks.*

10. Each group writes the rules it has formulated on the board. Use the explanations in **FYI**, on page 115, to correct the students' rules. Have groups correct their own examples by testing them against the rules.

11. [HMWK]. Ask students to record their examples on tape. To correct the tape, model only the mispronounced words. Ask the student to practice and re-record those words in isolation and in a sentence.

12. Go to **#53 Hearing the End.** Divide the class into five groups. Each group chooses five entries from the list, transliterates them, and indicates linking. When all have finished, discuss the entries as a class and practice them as a choral reading.

13. Each group then adds five new entries to its list, again transliterating and showing linking. As a class, discuss several from each group.

14. Using **#54 W6NTS16P7N16T13M** each group chooses at least five entries from **#53 Hearing the End** to write a short "Once upon a time . . ." story. After a brief rehearsal each group reads its story *in unison* to the class. This activity can be a competition for using the most phrases from **#53** or for the best unison reading.

#49 The Past Tense: *-ed*

The pronunciation of the past tense marker *-ed* depends on the sound that comes directly before the *-ed* ending. The three possible ways to pronounce *-ed* are

Use this column to collect examples and formulate rules.

| *-ed* ➞ /t/ | Diagram | /t/ Examples |
| | | Rule |

| *-ed* ➞ /d/ | Diagram | /d/ Examples |
| | | Rule |

| *-ed* ➞ /16d/ | Diagram | /16d/ Examples |
| | | Rule |

#50 Hearing the Past

Using some of your example words from **#49 The Past Tense: -ed**, write three sentences. Then speak them to your group. The other group members will tell you what they heard. Then you will check if it was OK, write what it should be or what it was. See examples 1 and 2.

My three sentences	Group comments	OK	Should be/was
1. I looked through the book.	2 people heard *lookt*/3 heard *look*		should be look*t* - make a stronger *t*
2. She petted the dog.	1 person heard *petteded*/all others heard *petted*	X	was P4D16D
3.			
4.			
5.			

Use the space below to make notes for commenting when you are monitoring the other members of your group.

#51 Back to the Past

Use the columns to practice the pronunciation of the sample words. Then enter additional practice words from your own occupation, profession, or interests in the appropriate column.

-ed → /t/	*-ed* → /d/	*-ed* → /16d/
chipped	damaged	dented
polished	sharpened	rusted
rushed	ordered	budgeted
worked	handled	located
stopped	tightened	recorded
iced	mildewed	melted
diagnosed	examined	tested
shopped	bargained	traded

#52 The -s Ending: Third Person Singular/Noun Plural

The pronunciation of the third person singular and the noun plural -s ending depends on the sound that comes directly before it. The three possible ways to pronounce the -s ending are

Use this column to collect examples and formulate rules.

-s → /s/	Diagram	/s/	Examples
			Rule

-s → /z/	Diagram	/z/	Examples
			Rule

-s → /16z/	Diagram	/16z/	Examples
			Rule

#53 Hearing the End

Phrases   **Transliteration and Linking**

peas in a pod

piece of cake

pieces of pizza

places I've been

books I've read

lots of time

passes the buck

foots the bill

bags of chips

boxes of disks

rooms in a house

cars on the road

maps, charts, and graphs

doctors, nurses, and dentists

The rug's on the floor.

She runs in the race.

He plays in the sand.

Add your own.

#54 W6NTS16P7N16T13M

Instructions: Choose a minimum of five phrases from among your group's entries. List them in the first column, then create a ''once upon a time . . .'' story around them. Write your final version below. Rehearse and prepare to read it in unison to the class.

Group phrases	Final version
	Once upon a time . . .

Lesson Twelve

Questions

1. The formation and intonation of questions remain problematic for many students. This lesson covers *yes/no,* information (*wh-*), and statement questions.

2. Begin with *yes/no* questions. Ask the class to generate some questions (ten or so is enough) that can be answered with a simple *yes* or *no* and write them on the board (*Are you hungry? Do they have a dog? Did you finish your homework? Is he married? Can you swim? Would you like some tea?*).

3. In small groups, students use these examples to derive the two grammar rules for forming *yes/no* questions. Use **#55 *Yes/No* Questions.** Discuss as a class.

4. Now model the typical intonation pattern for *yes/no* questions: rising intonation, with stress on the final content word in the sentence. The class repeats in unison.

   - *Do you have money?*   ↗
   - *Did they buy a house?*   ↗
   - *Did they go shopping?*   ↗

5. With the same sentences, shift the stressed word to change the meaning:

   - *Do you have money?*   ↗
   - *Did they buy a house?*   ↗
   - *Did they go shopping yesterday?* ↗

6. As a class, practice the examples on **#56 *Yes/No* Intonation.** Then in small groups, students write several original sentences. For each, they should show how changing the stressed word affects linking and meaning.

FYI

The rules for forming *yes/no* questions are as follows:

1. Move forms of *to be,* auxiliaries, and modals to the beginning of the sentence:

   - She is hungry.   ➡ Is she hungry?
   - We can cook.   ➡ Can we cook?
   - They were reading.   ➡ Were they reading?
   - You are going to study.   ➡ Are you going to study?
   - He will be there.   ➡ Will he be there?
   - She would have gone.   ➡ Would she have gone?
   - We have finished it.   ➡ Have we finished it?

2. With all other verbs, begin the sentence with

   - *do/does*   for present tense verbs
   - *did*   for simple past tense verbs

   and change the verb to the infinitive, omitting *to:*

   - He eats hamburgers every night.   ➡
     Does he eat hamburgers every night?
   - She went shopping yesterday.   ➡
     Did she go shopping yesterday?
   - They have a big dog.   ➡
     Do they have a big dog?

   Note the difference between *have* used as an auxiliary as opposed to its use as a verb showing possession.

---

7. Ask individual students to write a sentence on the board and say one variation of it. The other students give feedback on (1) which word was stressed and (2) the intended meaning of the sentence.

8. [HMWK]. Students write two or three additional sentences (original and variations of each) on **#56 *Yes/No* Intonation**, being sure to complete columns 2 and 3. They record the sentences and variations in the order written. Both **#56** and the tape are handed in.

9. Move on to information questions (also called *wh-* questions). Ask the class for examples of questions that cannot be answered with *yes* or *no*. Write them on the board. From these, derive the question words used to form information-seeking questions: *who, what, when, where, why, which, whose, how*. . . .

10. Divide the class into small groups so that each has at least one narrator, one listener, and one recorder. The narrator tells a two to three minute story, recounting an event or experience. The listener asks three to five *wh-* questions, and the recorder writes them down. At the end of three rounds (students changing roles each time) each group will have ten to fifteen questions, which are then written on the board. Put a check mark next to those questions that are grammatically correct.

11. Turn to **#57 Information Questions**. In small groups, students derive rules from the correct questions on the board. Groups report out and the rules are formulated as a class. Students then use the rules to correct the unmarked questions on the board.

12. Use the examples below to model the typical intonation pattern for information questions. It is the same as statement intonation, with stress on the final content word in the sentence. The class repeats in unison.

    • How much money do you have?
    • When's the homework due?
    • Where's the new restaurant?
    • Why didn't she tell him?
    • Whose bike did you borrow?

13. With the same sentences, shift the stressed word to change the meaning:

    • How much money do <u>you</u> have?
    • When's the homework <u>due</u>?
    • Where's the <u>new</u> restaurant?
    • Why <u>didn't</u> she tell him?
    • Whose bike did <u>you</u> borrow?

14. As a class, practice the examples on **#58 Information Questions: Intonation**. Students then write original sentences in pairs or individually.

15. Ask individual students to write a sentence on the board and say one variation of it. The other students give feedback on (1) which word was stressed and (2) the intended meaning of the sentence.

FYI

The question words (*who, what, when, where, why, which, whose, how*) are used to form information-seeking questions (also called *wh-* questions) in English.

The rules for forming information questions are:

1. The question word always begins the sentence.

2. Only *who* or *what* can be either the subject or object of a sentence. *When, where, why, which, whose,* and *how* can only be the object.*

3. When *who* and *what* are the subject of a sentence, the word order is the same as in a statement.

   - He ate the hot dog.
     Who ate the hot dog?
   - The book was on the table.
     What book was on the table?
   - They should have done the homework.
     Who should have done the homework?

   In all other cases, the question word is the object of the sentence.

4. When the question word is the object of the sentence the following pattern is used:
   Q word + *do/does/did* + subject + verb + modal
   forms of *to be*
   has/have†

She will call **him**.	I saw **them**.
Who(m) will she call?	**Who(m)** did you see?
They have done **it**.	He wants **a dog**.
What have they done?	**What** does he want?
I'm going to **the library**.	I want **that one**.
Where are you going?	**Which** (one) do you want?

We should be there **at noon**. **When** should we be there?	That book is **hers**. **Whose** (book) is it?
It's $6.00. **How** much is it?	We've been waiting for **an hour**. **How** long have you been waiting?
They couldn't/didn't **because** . . . **Why** couldn't/didn't they . . . ?	They couldn't/didn't **because** . . . **Why** couldn't/didn't they . . . ?

---

*Whose can be used both as a modifier or alone, e.g., *Whose dog is it? Whose is it?* Either way, it acts as an object. *Whom*, the object form of *who*, is becoming less frequent in informal English.

† Note the difference between *have* used as an auxiliary as opposed to its use as a verb showing possession.

16. [HMWK]. Students write additional sentences (original and variations of each) on **#58 Information Questions: Intonation,** being sure to complete columns 2 and 3. They record the sentences and variations in the order written. Both **#58** and the tape are handed in.

17. Next, move on to statement questions. Any statement can become a question through the use of rising intonation.

- You're doing your homework? ↗
- The dishes are done? ↗
- It's midnight already? ↗
- You'll be there by ten? ↗

This intonation pattern is used to confirm or show reactions such as surprise, doubt, or incredulity.

To question a specific part of a message, question words or phrases are used.

He said he'd do it **tomorrow**.	He said he'd do it *when*?
It looks like an **elephant**.	It looks like a *what*?
It's about 250 **miles**.	It's *how* far?

18. As a class, practice the first few examples on **#59 The Statement as Question.** Students then pair off to practice the remaining examples. Each pair then writes six more statements and corresponding questions and practices them, taking turns reading the statement and the question. Each pair models one or two of its statements-into-questions to the class for unison repetition.

19. [HMWK]. Students write and record all three types of questions: yes/no, information, and statement questions. They follow the instructions on **#60 Three Question Types** and turn in this worksheet along with their tape. A critique section is provided at the bottom of the page. Record the sentences that need additional work for the student to use as a model for practice.

20. Turn to **#61 Comprehensibility Quotient.** Again, ask students to mark where they fit on the chart. Remind them that they may use nonwhole numbers, e.g. 2.75. Students hand in the forms. Compare them with the self-ratings done on the first day of class (**#1 Comprehensibility Quotient**) and return both. You may wish to add your own rating and/or use these forms as a basis for grading.

#55 *Yes / No* Questions

List ten of the *yes/no* questions generated by the class.

1.   6.

2.   7.

3.   8.

4.   9.

5.   10.

Formation

Use the questions above to figure out the two grammar rules for forming *yes/no* questions.

Rule one:

Rule two:

#56 *Yes / No* Intonation

Use the examples below to practice shifting stress to change meaning. Then, write some of your own *yes/no* questions and practice shifting the stress to change your meaning.

1. Question	2. Stress, linking, reduction, and deletion	3. Intended meaning
1. Is he arriving today?	Is he *arriving* today?	asking about the activity in general
	Is he arriving *today*?	focusing specifically on *time*
	Is *he* arriving today?	focusing specifically on *him*

#57 Information Questions

Record ten of the questions generated by the class.

1.   6.

2.   7.

3.   8.

4.   9.

5.   10.

Formation

Use the above sentences to figure out the rule for forming information questions. To derive the rule, answer the following two questions:
1. Where do you put the question word in the sentence?
2. What follows the question word?

The rule is

#58 Information Questions: Intonation

Create two original information questions. Then shift the stress to different words to change the meaning.

1. Question	2. Stress, linking, reduction, and deletion	3. Intended meaning
1. What's he doing?	What's he *doing?*	asking about his activity
	What's *he* doing?	focus is on *him,* not her, us, etc.

#59 The Statement as Question

Make statements into questions by
  • using a rising intonation pattern or
  • using a question word or phrase for emphasis.
Practice with the examples first. Then create your own.

Speaker A's question	Speaker B's question
1. Dinner's ready.	Dinner's ready?
2. I'm not finished yet.	You're not finished yet?
3. You have high blood pressure.	I have high blood pressure?
4. Your car needs a new clutch.	I need a new clutch?
5. I'm sorry, we're out of coffee.	You're out of coffee?
6. The test will have 200 questions.	The test will have *how many* questions?
7. The rent is $575 plus utilities.	The rent is *how much?*
8. You'll have to have a root canal in about two weeks.	I'll have to have a *what?* I'll have to have a root canal *when?*
9. The company's sending you to Disneyland for two weeks.	You're sending me *where?*
10. The traffic was terrible. It took me two hours to get home!	It took you *how long?*

11.

12.

13.

14.

15.

#60 Three Question Types

Name _____ Date _____

Write three questions under each category. Record each one twice, shifting the stress to change the meaning.

Yes/No questions

1.

2.

3.

Information questions

1.

2.

3.

Statement questions

1.

2.

3.

Teacher's critique

	Rating				Comments
Grammar	1	2	3	4	
Stress shift	1	2	3	4	
Intonation	1	2	3	4	

In addition, review lesson(s) / chart(s)

Overall rating   1   2   3   4

#61 Comprehensibility Quotient

Rating	Description	Impact on communication
1.0	Speech is reasonably intelligible, but pronunciation or grammatical errors distract listener; repetitions and verifications are frequently required.	Accent causes frequent interference with communication; significant listener effort required.
2.0	Speech is largely intelligible; pronunciation or grammar errors are obvious, but repetition and verification are less frequently required.	Accent causes interference primarily at the distraction level; listener's attention is often diverted from the content to focus instead on the novelty of the speech pattern.
3.0	Speech is fully intelligible; variances from native speaker norm are present, but repetition and verification are seldom required.	Accent causes little interference; speech is fully functional for effective communication; minimal listener effort required.
4.0	Speech is near native; only minor features of divergence from native speaker can be detected.	Accent causes no interference. Speech is fully comprehensible; no listener effort required.

Student's name _____

Native language _____

Self-Rating _____   Date _____

Adapted from Joan Morley, *Intensive Consonant Pronunciation Practice* (Ann Arbor: University of Michigan Press, 1992).

And Finally . . .

The Abbott and Costello routine is about the players on a baseball team. Before turning to the routine itself, we suggest the following activity.

1. The students who know the most about baseball begin to explain how the game is played. Other students ask *yes/no,* information, and statement questions to learn more. Each questioner must announce the type of question he or she will ask before actually asking it. The remaining class members correct the question (if necessary) before one of the "experts" gives the answer. For example, the conversation could go as follows: (*BE* designates the baseball experts, *SQ* designates a student-questioner, and *CM* designates one of the other class members).

    SQ: I'm going to ask a *yes/no* question: Does the catcher can hit the ball?

137

CM: That's a *yes/no* question, but it's not right; it should be
         "Can the catcher hit the ball?" or "Does the catcher hit the
         ball?"
SQ: O.K. Can the catcher hit the ball?
BE: No, the catcher can't hit the ball.
SQ: How many players are on a team?
CM: You didn't say what type of question you're asking.
SQ: Oh, right. It's an information question.
BE: There are nine players on a team.
SQ: This is a statement question. There are only nine?
CM: Sounds fine.
BE: That's right, only nine per team play at a time.
SQ: This is an information question. Why there aren't women
         players?
CM: Sounds fine.
Teacher: Whoops, just a minute. Let's think about that one again:
         Why there aren't women players? What word order do we
         use for information questions?
CM: Oh, why aren't there women players?
BE: Wow, that's a hard one! Maybe our teacher knows . . .

2. Have the class listen to portions of *Who's on First* without looking at the
   script.*

3. Listen to the tape a second time; students follow the script.

4. Ask the class to identify what is causing confusion in the portion of the
   routine you have listened to and why it is humorous. For instance, on the
   first page:

   • Costello starts with a long *yes/no* question (line 1).
   • The humor is foreshadowed by Abbott's comment that ballplayers have
     "very peculiar names" (line 2).
   • This is followed by a statement question by Costello (line 3).
   • In line 6, Abbott lays the foundation for the humor by giving the names
     of the first, second, and third basemen.
   • Line 9 contains another statement question.
   • Lines 11, 19, and 21 contain information questions.

---

* The script has been edited for use with this text, but the deletions will not interfere if you are using
the recording. If a recording is not available, have two native speakers read the script to the class.

- Intonation contributes to the misunderstandings in lines 8, 14, 16, 18, and 20.

Students might want to talk about similar types of humor in their native languages.

5. As a final activity, divide the routine into as many segments as you have pairs of students. Assign one segment to each pair. After marking stress, linking, and intonation, each pair practices its segment. Finally, the pairs read their segment to the class in order, to recreate the routine.

If the equipment is available, video- or audiotape this exercise. Recording not only provides feedback to the students but also gives them a chance to have fun with English.

Who's on First?

(edited for listening classes)

1 Costello: Will you tell me the guys' names on the baseball team so when I go to see them in the ball park I'll be able to know those fellows? I wanna find out the fellows' names. I'm crazy about baseball.

2 Abbott: All right. But you know, strange as it may seem, they give ball players nowadays very peculiar names.

3 C: Funny names?

4 A: Nicknames. Nicknames.

5 C: Not—not as funny as my name . . .

6 A: Oh, absolutely. Yes. Now, on this baseball team we have Who's on first, What's on second, I Don't Know is on third . . .

7 C: That's what I want to find out. I want you to tell me the names of the fellows on the team.

8 A: I'm telling you. Who's on first, What's on second, I Don't Know is on third . . .

9 C: You know the fellows' names?

10 A: Yes.

11 C: Well then, who's playin' first?

12 A: Yes.

13 C: I mean the fellow's name on first base.

14 A: Who.

15 C: The fellow playin' first base for the team.

16 A: Who.

17 C: The guy on first base.

18	A:	Who is on first.
19	C:	Well, what are you askin' me for?
20	A:	I'm not asking you, I'm telling you. *Who is on first.*
21	C: -	I'm asking you—who's on first?
22	A:	That's the man's name!
23	C:	That's whose name?
24	A:	Yes.
25	C:	Well, go ahead and tell me!
26	A:	Who.
27	C:	The guy on first.
28	A:	Who.
29	C:	The first baseman.
30	A:	Who is on first.
31	C:	Have you got a first baseman on first?
32	A:	Certainly.
33	C:	Then who's playing first?
34	A:	Absolutely.
35	C:	When you pay off the first baseman every month, who gets the money?
36	A:	Every dollar of it. And why not, the man's entitled to it.
37	C:	Who is?
38	A:	Yes.
39	C:	So who gets it?
40	A:	Why shouldn't he? Sometimes his wife comes down and collects it.
41	C:	Whose wife?
42	A:	Yes. After all, the man earns it.
43	C:	Who does?
44	A:	Absolutely.
45	C:	Well, all I'm trying to find out is what's the guy's name on first base.
46	A:	Oh no, no. What is on second base.
47	C:	I'm not asking you who's on second.
48	A:	Who's on first.
49	C:	That's what I'm trying to find out.
50	A:	Well, don't change the players around.
51	C:	I'm not changing nobody.
52	A:	Now take it easy!
53	C:	What's the guy's name on first base?
54	A:	What's the guy's name on second base.
55	C:	I'm not askin' you who's on second.
56	A:	Who's on first.
57	C:	I don't know.
58	A:	He's on third. We're not talkin' about him.

59	C:	How could I get on third base?
60	A:	You mentioned his name.
61	C:	If I mentioned the third baseman's name, who did I say is playing third?
62	A:	No, Who's playing first.
63	C:	Stay offa first, will ya?
64	A:	Well what do you want me to do?
65	C:	Now what's the guy's name on first base?
66	A:	What's on second.
67	C:	I'm not asking ya who's on second.
68	A:	Who's on first.
69	C:	I don't know.
70	A:	He's on third.
71	C:	There I go back on third again.
72	A:	Well, I can't change their names.
73	C:	Say, will you please stay on third base.
74	A:	Please. Now what is it you want to know?
75	C:	What is the fellow's name on third base?
76	A:	What is the fellow's name on second base.
77	C:	I'm not askin' ya who's on second.
78	A:	Who's on first.
79	C:	I don't know.
80	A and C:	Third base!
81	C:	You got an outfield?
82	A:	Oh, sure.
83	C:	This team's got a good outfield?
84	A:	Oh, absolutely.
85	C:	The left fielder's name?
86	A:	Why.
87	C:	I don't know, I just thought I'd ask.
88	A:	Well, I just thought I'd tell you.
89	C:	Then tell me who's playing left field.
90	A:	Who's playing first.
91	C:	Stay out of the infield.
92	A:	Don't mention any names out here.
93	C:	I want to know what's the fellow's name in left field.
94	A:	What is on second.
95	C:	I'm not asking you who's on second.
96	A:	Who is on first.
97	C:	I don't know.
98	A and C:	Third base!
99	A:	Now take it easy, take it easy man.
100	C:	And the left fielder's name?
101	A:	Why.
102	C:	Because.

103 A: Oh he's center field. He's center.
104 C: Center field.
105 A: Now look, please.
106 C: Mr. Abbott.
107 A: Yes.
108 C: Wait a minute. You got a pitcher on the team?
109 A: Wouldn't this be a fine team without a pitcher.
110 C: I don't know. Tell me the pitcher's name.
111 A: Tomorrow.
112 C: You don't want to tell me today?
113 A: I'm telling you, man.
114 C: Then go ahead.
115 A: Tomorrow.
116 C: What time?
117 A: What time what?
118 C: What time tomorrow are you gonna tell me who's pitching?
119 A: Now listen, Who is not pitching. Who is on . . .
120 C: I'll break your arm if you say who's on first.
121 A: Then why come up here and ask?
122 C: I want to know what's the pitcher's name.
123 A: What's on second.
124 C: I don't know.
125 A and C: Third base!
126 C: You got a catcher?
127 A: Yes.
128 C: The catcher's name?
129 A: Today.
130 C: And Tomorrow's pitching.
131 A: Now you've got it.